THE DEACON

The Deacon

Icon of Christ the Servant, Minister of the Threshold

TIM O'DONNELL

Paulist Press
New York / Mahwah, NJ

Unless an English-language work or translation is cited in the footnote to a quotation, all translations in the text and notes are by the author. This includes translations from the New Testament, patristic sources, conciliar documents, papal and other church documents, modern sources, and secondary works.

Cover image by Naumov S / Shutterstock.com
Cover and book design by Lynn Else

Library of Congress Cataloging-in-Publication Data
Names: O'Donnell, Tim, author
Title: The deacon : icon of Christ the servant, minister of the threshold / Tim O'Donnell.
Description: New York : Paulist Press, 2020. | Includes bibliographical references and index.
Summary: "The Deacon develops a vision of the distinctive ministerial identity of deacons that is theologically rigorous and practically useful, combining two complementary images: 'icon of Christ the servant' and 'minister of the threshold.'"— Provided by publisher.
Identifiers: LCCN 2019043683 (print) | LCCN 2019043684 (ebook) | ISBN 9780809154258 (paperback) | ISBN 9781587688102 (ebook)
Subjects: LCSH: Deacons—Catholic Church.
Classification: LCC BX1912 .O36 2020 (print) | LCC BX1912 (ebook) | DDC 262/.142—dc23
LC record available at https://lccn.loc.gov/2019043683
LC ebook record available at https://lccn.loc.gov/2019043684

ISBN 978-0-8091-5425-8 (paperback)
ISBN 978-1-58768-810-2 (e-book)

Published by Paulist Press
997 Macarthur Boulevard
Mahwah, New Jersey 07430
www.paulistpress.com

Printed and bound in the
United States of America

For Elke, with abiding love and gratitude

CONTENTS

Contents

ACKNOWLEDGMENTS

A book like this one, which combines theological reflection with the empirical and practical study of ministry, necessarily benefits from influences, encounters, experiences, support, and guidance from persons too numerous to name. Here I can only mention a few of the many to whom I feel profound gratitude for helping me to formulate the ideas developed in the book. My historical study of the diaconate began fifteen years ago under the guidance of John W. O'Malley and Francine Cardman. Richard W. Lennan was instrumental in helping me to locate diaconal ministry in the theological conversation. St. Peter Parish, Cambridge, Massachusetts—the pastor, Fr. Leonard O'Malley, the staff, and the community—provided a fertile ground for learning about practical ministry during my seven-year assignment there. Richard Gaillardetz and John F. Baldovin read all or sections of the manuscript and provided many insightful suggestions, as did my fellow deacons Christopher Connelly, Thomas O'Shea, and Fran Burke. As always, my wife, Elke, was an unfailing source of inspiration and support.

Tim O'Donnell
Cambridge, Massachusetts
Feast of St. Lawrence, 2019

• • • • • •

CHAPTER ONE

WHO ARE THESE DEACONS AND WHAT DO THEY DO?

In the fifty years since St. Paul VI gave official sanction for a permanent diaconate in the Roman Catholic Church, the number of deacons has grown rapidly, from zero to more than forty-six thousand worldwide.[1] This impressive arithmetic should not obscure the fact that the diaconate has grown up haltingly and unevenly in the worldwide Church. The great majority of deacons are found in North America and in certain countries of Western Europe. Elsewhere, in general, the diaconate is either lightly planted or unknown.[2] Yet even in those regions where this ministry has taken root, there remains widespread confusion about who deacons are and what the Church ordains them to do. The lack of any well-defined, commonly shared understanding is found among priests, bishops, professional nonordained ministers, church volunteers, and people in the pews, not to mention the many—Catholics and non-Catholics— who rub shoulders with deacons in the workplace and other nonchurch settings.

The confusion is hardly surprising. In the life of the Catholic Church, fifty years barely count as a moment; yesterday there were no deacons in permanent ministry, and today they are cropping up, in some places at least, more and more. People begin to notice that they help out at the parish and have some

1

sacramental functions. Yet most, whether inside or outside the church—and this includes many priests and bishops—have not had enough sustained personal experience of deacons in ministry to come away with a clear mental picture of their distinctive ministerial identity and purpose.

Nor has the diaconate taken on a public face that might serve to make its outlines clearer. Despite their rapidly increasing numbers, deacons have not been the subject of headlines, not even in reports about Catholic ministry, where popes, cardinals, bishops, and priests have drawn almost all of the attention.[3] The relative invisibility of deacons is easy to understand. Their ministry is not glamorous; it is exercised far from clerical authority and, so far (thank God), they have steered clear almost entirely of public scandal. In addition, deacons in their typical North American and European context usually are not pastoral ministry professionals: most deacons earn their living outside the church settings where they minister, and functionally act as volunteers. No wonder many people do not see their newfound presence in the Church as important enough to warrant any real effort at understanding what is distinctive about their ministry. Yet every year, in the typical Western context where the diaconate has taken root, we see more deacons in the ministry. At the same time, the numbers of priests, and, in many regions, of regular churchgoers as well, have continued to decline. The Spirit seems to be speaking here: the diaconate has some gift to offer the Church of the present and the future.

The lack of a widely understood ministerial identity is a problem for deacons themselves, though through formation programs, preached retreats, their own prayer and reflection, and the sacrament of ordination itself, they have some concepts and experiences to work with. Most have a sense that the diaconate is about service—to the Church and its mission, to the people in the pews, to the suffering and marginalized. Yet how do these different kinds of service get integrated among the many needs that call upon an active ministry? And how might they come together as the defining quality of an ordained office, given that all Christians are called to service? Going further, diaconal service is often associated with the idea that deacons somehow should represent Christ the servant, a metaphor often invoked but rarely examined and somehow supposed to be connected with humble service and charity.[4] Finally, given their involvement through work and family in everyday secular life, most deacons feel that they should represent the Church in the wider world while also bringing a distinct perspective from life in that world into their preaching and pastoral ministry. Yet how, in everyday life, does one do this? These questions have proved hard to work out in ways that are both intelligible and useful.

Then we have the "doing" part of diaconal identity: What are deacons particularly supposed to do, and why? Diaconal service is said to include the three "tasks" given to the diaconate by its foundational document at Vatican II, *Lumen Gentium*: the ministries of word, liturgy, and charity.[5] What these tasks consist of and how they relate to each other, either in an individual's ministry or in giving purpose to the office of deacon as a grade of holy orders, are matters most deacons would have difficulty explaining in a direct, practical way that is also grounded both in Church teaching and good theology.

This book takes up the challenge posed by this widespread confusion and fleshes out an account of diaconal identity, of who deacons are and what they are tasked to do. We use two models: Christ the servant and minister of the threshold. The models give goals and guidelines to deacons in ministry. Deacons, for their part, are called to represent these models or, as we sometimes hear, be icons of them, for the Church and the world. Fortunately, the basic thinking behind the two models is not original to this book. We already find such ideas applied to deacons within Church documents, theological essays, popular magazine articles, diocesan websites, and practical handbooks. The appeal to Christ the servant crops up everywhere. The threshold model builds upon a widespread perception about diaconal ministry, sometimes formulated using words like *threshold* and *borderland* for the locus of that ministry, sometimes presenting the deacon as a kind a bridge or mediating figure. Here deacons are seen as ministering from a kind of in-between place: between clergy and laity, or between the Church and the broader society. In fact, the general images of Christ the servant, and of some kind of threshold minister, come up so often precisely because they say something significant, and indeed foundational, about who deacons are and what the Church is calling them to do. Thus, the basic content of these two models is already, to varying degrees, part of the self-understanding of deacons today. However, the theological literature has neither examined the two themes with the rigor they deserve, nor offered them as complementary aspects of a full diaconal identity with practical applications. Those are the tasks undertaken here.

This book is designed to meet the needs of two sets of readers who in some measure overlap. One group is committed to the theological disciplines and requires an account of diaconal ministry that is coherent and conceptually precise enough to participate in theological conversations about ministry, the Church, or the sacrament of holy orders. The second set of readers has a more practical focus. They include deacons practicing ministry, or anyone discerning a call to the office, or those in formation for ordination. Other readers with this more practical interest are the people who oversee, teach, form, mentor, collaborate with, or in any way interact with deacons. That interaction, in turn, may be in diaconate formation programs, parishes, workplaces, or families. Finally, anyone watching this ministry grow and expand in today's Church will benefit from a practical knowledge of who these ministers are and what the Church is calling them to do. This second set of readers requires an account of the diaconate that is theologically solid but also provides models for practice in real ministry situations. This book directly addresses their needs. It's style and the content are aimed throughout at the two audiences simultaneously. Indeed, the subject matter itself requires us to satisfy both sets of readers, since any treatment of ministerial identity must meet the twin tests of theological coherence and practical usefulness. Accordingly, the text in the book is as nontechnical as possible, and discussion of competing views that do not contribute significantly to the main argument may be found in the endnotes, together with citations of the pertinent literature.

THE THEOLOGICAL CONVERSATION

As deacons have responded to a variety of pastoral and mission needs, their experiences have sparked a large body of writing reflecting on the practical shape of this ministry on the ground.[6] At the same time, particularly over the past twenty-five years, a steady stream of Church documents and theological writing has given both volume and sophistication to the theological conversation about the diaconate. The very fact that the discussion is active and ongoing suggests that we still have important things to learn, both theological and practical, about this important office in the Church. Yet the conversation also has reached a certain maturity that was lacking even a decade ago.

This maturity does not mean that there is any broad agreement around a particular definition of diaconal identity. Most studies about the diaconate shine light on one or another element in this identity but are too brief or narrowly focused to consider that identity in full.[7] Others cover a broad terrain but come to only tentative or rather general conclusions.[8] Still others put forth somewhat speculative new approaches without incorporating the valuable insights of earlier proposals that have theological weight and are already rooted to some extent in the everyday self-understanding of many deacons.[9] The theological conversation about the diaconate, though broad and deep, turns out to be surprisingly fragmented.

This fragmentation has frustrated attempts to address adequately the central and urgent question about who deacons are and what they are called to do. As we have already noted, a worthy answer must be both theologically coherent and practically useful. On the theological side, we must define in a rigorous manner how this office is sacramental and in what way it offers something distinctive within the Church's ministries. On the practical side, deacons themselves, along with those who form and supervise them, should find an account of diaconal identity that is concrete and intelligible enough to provide solid guidance for the practice of ministry. Although such a vision has not been developed fully anywhere in the voluminous writings

5

about the diaconate, that literature does give us a solid grounding and an excellent set of tools for the task.

This book builds upon the large tradition of writing about the diaconate that goes back over sixty-five years, beginning with the movement that took shape after World War II, seeking to revive the early Church office of deacon for contemporary needs. The two complementary models developed here, Christ the servant and minister of threshold, have significant support within that tradition of thought. In the current state of theological conversation, however, these models need rigorous analysis and, if they prove coherent and useful, a response to any criticisms.

THE STRUCTURE OF THIS BOOK

This book undertakes that analysis and response, proceeding as follows. After retrieving some foundational perspectives about the diaconate in the New Testament and in two of the earliest Church fathers (chapter 2), we will show how images of diaconal identity, including the two examined here, began to crystallize in the movement to revive the diaconate before and during Vatican II (chapters 3 through 5). Chapter 6 surveys explorations of diaconal identity since the council, noting that the threshold model, despite some suggestive explorations, dropped into the background, while that of Christ the servant became dominant and also attracted criticism. Chapter 7 begins the systematic treatment of diaconal identity by presenting a view of the office of deacon in its totality, integrating functional, relational, and sacramental dimensions. We then turn to the models themselves (chapters 8 and 9), showing how each one is rooted in the structure of a deacon's office and expresses something truly distinctive about the diaconate among the ministries of the Church. We also note how, taken together, the models are complementary and mutually reinforcing; and indeed, how they constitute the two halves of a single, complete, and authentic ministerial identity for deacons. Chapter 10 examines what light the models shed on the practice of diaconal ministry, including questions of vocation, ministry assignments, and personal discernment. Chapter 11 pulls the various conclusions of the book together and looks to the future, considering how some potential developments in ministry could affect the models and their use. The models, and the ministerial identity they guide and express, emerge as remarkably resilient in the face of possible changes.

THE CONTEXT OF DIACONAL MINISTRY

The diaconate has a very definite real-world context. Yet with the exception of empirical studies, the theological literature about diaconal ministry generally refers only to practical issues that have happened to have surfaced in the writer's own experience.[10] But ministers are real people operating within particular institutional, cultural, social, and interpersonal contexts. Theological reflection on any ministry, even when the surface argument is about (for example) the finer points of sacramental theology, always has a context, a framework given by real-life experience, which is assumed if not explicitly addressed.[11]

The institutional context considered here is the Roman Catholic permanent diaconate that was proposed by the Second Vatican Council, inaugurated by Pope St. Paul VI in 1967, and thereafter implemented unevenly throughout the worldwide Church. That is what is meant throughout this book by "the diaconate." The Eastern Catholic, Orthodox, Anglican, and Protestant diaconates, though they also can be "permanent," have a different history and ecclesial context, and therefore lie outside our scope.[12] Nor will we consider the transitional diaconate that leads to priesthood. Although this office has the same ordination rite as the permanent diaconate, the transitional office has a completely different history, ecclesial context, and ministerial self-understanding that together place it outside our study. (Chapter 11 will address the challenge to the development of a full diaconal identity posed by the parallel existence of two different diaconates.) As a further clarification, the office examined here will refer to the diaconate in its present canonical discipline, as restricted to men (and accordingly masculine pronouns will be used for convenience). In Chapter 11, when considering whether possible future developments would require any change in this book's models of diaconal identity, we conclude that they could be applied to women deacons, should the Church decide to ordain them. In fact, the diaconal identity that the models define provides no explicit support for either side of this currently debated issue, as we will see.

The diaconate has developed over the past fifty years in a clearly identifiable geographical context: North America and certain countries of Western Europe. Accordingly, this setting provides the typical context for deacons.[13] The geography dictates three conditions that affect their ministerial identity. First, within the Church itself, the diaconate has grown up alongside a rapid drop in the number of priests, together with a significant increase in ministerial activities by people who are not ordained, and who perform these functions on an occasional or full-time basis.[14] Accordingly, the diaconate must be clearly distinguished from priesthood, even as deacons take on certain sacramental and pastoral functions that until recent times usually were performed solely by priests. At the same time, diaconal identity must have something distinctive compared with that of nonordained ministers, particularly those who are professionally trained and hold responsible positions in the Church.

Second, the vast majority of deacons are married and employed in nonchurch jobs. Even if they are widowed or retired from such employment, this has been their defining situation for much of their lives. These characteristics of a deacon's social location are so prevalent that they can be treated as typical, as conditions of his ministerial life and action. There are exceptions, of course: unmarried deacons, and those who have always worked in church settings or church-affiliated organizations. But the typical case is so preponderant that it poses a set of challenges the diaconate has urgently needed to address, such as the practical balancing and sacramental relation between marriage and ordained office, or how to integrate the diaconate's particular dual focus, both inside the Church and within the wider world.

Finally, the culture and outlook of North America and Western Europe, the typical locus of diaconal ministry, can be described as increasingly post-Christian and indeed nonreligious. This situation differs markedly from some other regions of the world where, for example, Christianity may be the faith of a surviving minority, or make up one of several vibrant religious traditions that may be in competition or conflict. The cultural phenomenon of the West is a challenge calling for an imaginative response from all Christians and all ministers, but it presents particular challenges and opportunities for deacons, particularly as compared with bishops and priests, because deacons live in a distinctive in-between situation as committed Church ministers embedded in the secular world.

These three contextual characteristics of diaconal ministry (in the Church, in society, and in culture) are clearly identifiable and show no signs of changing in the foreseeable future. As a result, our study both can and must address this context as we inquire whether, or in what sense, deacons should be icons of Christ the servant and ministers of the threshold.

The office of deacon, of course, crystallized in a different context—that of the early Church. The participants at Vatican II sought to "revive" or "restore" that office to meet the pastoral and missionary needs of the later twentieth century. The next chapter examines some roots of that revival.

CHAPTER TWO

• • • • • • •

WITNESS FROM THE EARLY CHURCH

The office of deacon has a continuous history in the Church going back to New Testament times. The diaconate's functions and its relation to other ministries, especially those of bishops and priests, have gone through important transformations during these nearly two thousand years, so history does not provide us with any single model for the office. Yet the contemporary diaconate must have some kind of continuity with this long history; otherwise, why call someone a deacon?

The diaconate in the early Church, while not providing a precise model for today, nevertheless has a particular significance for this ministry. The first centuries were foundational for the Church, and the writings about the diaconate from that time carry the authority of the New Testament itself and of important Church fathers. Moreover, in the early Church, deacons exercised a vital and important ministry. Although the office later declined and became merely a step on the road to priesthood, the early Church provides a necessary witness to the diaconate as a permanent ministry.

Despite scholarly debates, certain broad outlines of the early diaconate are clear enough. Deacons, like other Church ministers, typically were married, and the deacons had a distinct ministry with a variety of functions. These were not the same everywhere and at all times, but generally included assisting presiders at community assemblies, distributing aid to the needy, and in some cases catechesis or financial administration. Church orders from the third century onward show them being ordained, like bishops and priests.[1] A full profile of ancient deacons would extend far beyond these brief indications, and fortunately there is a large historical literature on the early diaconate, either considered in itself or within broader studies of the Church's ministries during the first several centuries. Historians seek to reconstruct the functions of the office and its place among the various Church ministries. We need not go over the same ground here.[2] The historical accounts are widely available, and new ones continue to appear.[3]

For our purposes, however, the question remains: What relevance does the ancient diaconate have for diaconal identity today? Vatican II (1962–65) provides a basic answer: by stating that it was "restoring" the diaconate as a permanent ministry, the council affirmed that there is some kind of continuity between the ancient and the "restored" diaconates.[4] But to understand what kind of continuity, we must study the modern office itself, and this office now has its own history, covering the past sixty-five years or so, beginning with movement for a permanent diaconate that gathered steam soon after 1945. The story continues in the teaching of Vatican II and subsequent Church documents, in the ministry of deacons within our modern context, and in theological explorations of the diaconate up to the present. This is the history that defines the ministerial identity of deacons today. The next three chapters will cover this formative history.

Because of the foundational character of the early Church, however, the writings from that time—the New Testament and the Church fathers—continue to be a touchstone and guide for reflection about diaconal ministry today. Accordingly, this chapter, rather than attempting another historical reconstruction of the ancient diaconate, engages a selection of those writings, examining some key texts from the New Testament and from the early Church fathers Sts. Ignatius of Antioch (35–107) and Polycarp of Smyrna (69–155). Before turning to the texts, however, we need to look more closely at the historical question posed by diaconal office, and at how the emergence of the diaconate in modern times has reset the terms of that question.

GRAPPLING WITH HISTORY BEFORE VATICAN II

In the late 1940s and 1950s, when the movement for the diaconate as a permanent ministry was gathering strength, the proponents needed to find historical precedents because the proposal to make the diaconate permanent and open to married men required a significant change, both in the practice and in the theology of ministry. The office of deacon as it then existed in the Western Church was merely a transitional stage for celibate men on the road to priesthood, a stage that might last a few months or days—or even minutes, in the case of successive ordinations in a single rite. The office had some functions at Mass, but no independent ministerial purpose. The transitional diaconate is still a rite of passage today for those heading toward ordination as priests; the diaconal period, often a year now, is a time usually devoted to practical training for the priesthood. By the middle of the twentieth century the transitional diaconate for celibate men had been the sole norm in the Western Church for over a thousand years, universally practiced except in a few exceptional cases, where men ordained to the diaconate ended up not going on to the priesthood for one reason or another. Considered as a vehicle for ministry, the diaconate was an empty shell. The founders of a new movement for a permanent diaconate proposed to fill it with new life and purpose.

For that effort to be credible, historians needed to leapfrog the past millennium or more and find patterns of diaconal ministry in the ancient Church that supported the reform proposal. In doing so, they would participate in a broader intellectual current that motivated some influential scholars in the pre-Vatican II generation to go "back to the sources," particularly the Bible and the Church fathers, to discover what the contemporary Church might be able to retrieve for its theology, self-understanding, and pastoral needs.[5] Scholars like Jean Lécuyer, Walter Croce, and Jean Colson produced significant historical studies along these lines during the 1940s and 1950s, documenting that the ancient diaconate was a permanent and significant ministry.[6]

Proponents of a modern diaconate needed to grapple with the full history of the diaconate for three reasons. First, as already noted, neither current practice nor the history of the past millennium provided support for their proposal. Second, because the office itself had a continuous existence from the early Church to the present, the history, as a whole, both imposed limitations and suggested possibilities for a diaconate adapted to modern needs. This becomes clear by comparison with other ministries in the Church. Over the centuries, there have been many ecclesiastical offices, from abbots to vicars general, and many significant jobs, from chancellors to pastoral associates, that are recognizably ministerial and can be defined in any way that Church leaders find appropriate. Proponents of a modern diaconate were not so free; the office had the weight of some nineteen hundred years of history that conditioned how the diaconate might develop in the present.

Third, the diaconate generally was understood as a grade of holy orders; this situation required a justification grounded in sacramental theology for any possible changes in the office, and thereby complicated decisions about such changes.[7] The sacrament of orders, also conferred on bishops and priests of course, had its own history of development and change. Particularly since the Middle Ages, the sacrament had come to be almost solely identified with priesthood; the sacramental rationale for the diaconate, and indeed for the episcopacy, had become obscured.[8] But ancient Church documents gave evidence of the ordination of deacons, and indeed married deacons, to a permanent ministry.

Historians and theologians before the council succeeded in bringing the ancient diaconate alive and presenting it as a foundational model for the pastoral and mission needs of the mid-twentieth century. The fact that the historians framed their questions about the early Church amid modern concerns does not mean they failed to work critically with the sources or to reconstruct the most accurate possible picture of the ancient diaconate. They did so, demonstrating that the office was a distinct, permanent, and ordained ministry in the early Church. The council, for its part, accepted this historical foundation and framed the proposed diaconate as a restoration. Today it is no longer necessary, for an understanding of diaconal identity, to scour the early Church sources for historical precedents, as interesting as these might be.[9] More fruitful for an understanding of diaconal identity is an engagement with this foundational period through the witness of texts.

WITNESS FROM THE EARLY CHURCH

How do we reflect fruitfully on the diaconate by engaging the early Church through some of its texts? The method here is not, as in historical analysis, a critical reconstruction of who ancient deacons were and what they did. Rather, the focus is on the texts themselves, and what they can tell us about diaconal ministry, if close attention is paid to their language, structure, style, and cultural setting. A careful exegesis of the chosen passages in their original language and context serves as a control against the danger of reading in our own reality, while enabling us to discover themes in the texts that are fruitful for our own reflection. In this kind of interpretation, the texts are not exposed to historical criticism ("What actually happened?"), and it is not necessary to decide whether the texts are telling us how things actually were or whether they are describing an idealized situation that the author puts forward as a goal.[10] The texts can guide us equally well in either case.

Our approach here is frankly selective. Besides making no pretense of constructing a historical portrait of the ancient diaconate, this chapter does not seek to synthesize any broad theology of the office based on the New Testament and the Church fathers. Instead, two key passages from the New Testament, 1 Timothy 3:1–13 and Acts 6:1–6, will be examined in detail for the light they shed on the qualities and functions of diaconal office. These two text-based reflections are sandwiched between an overview of New Testament models of ministry and a brief consideration of how the early Church fathers Ignatius and Polycarp point toward diaconal office as exemplifying Christ the servant. For the two New Testament passages, this chapter presents the basic interpretation, leaving translations of the texts and the more technical exegesis to appendices 1 and 2.

MINISTRY AS A RESPONSE TO NEED IN THE NEW TESTAMENT

If we begin by surveying the New Testament in its entirety, the most striking impression that emerges about ministry is how flexibly it develops in response to rapidly changing missionary and pastoral needs. A brief and admittedly incomplete summary suffices to show this. Christ himself commissions the Twelve as an apostolic leadership for the Church, and this leadership quickly extends itself in a remarkable diversity of forms.[11] Thus, we see the commissioning of the Seventy and the Seven, and the incorporation of Paul, James, Barnabas, Timothy, and others into the leadership both as apostles and apostolic delegates. In the churches founded by Paul and his successors, we hear of a wide diversity of ministries, understood as charisms, or gifts, of the Holy Spirit. These include prophets, teachers, healers, speakers in tongues, and those who provide financial support. We also find the development of ministerial office by *episkopoi*, *presbyteroi*, and *diakonoi*, the offices or titles that eventually become bishops, presbyters/priests, and deacons.[12]

This New Testament account of a flexible development of ministry responding to pastoral and mission needs comes from a unique and unrepeatable phase in the life of the Church. Taken as a model, this account cannot be pressed to support limitless experimentation. Nor can or should the ministerial practices of the early Church be copied slavishly for another time. But these scriptural texts do offer a useful model for adapting ministry to contemporary needs. The New Testament itself, then, provides support for the impulse that envisioned the diaconate as a permanent ministry in the mid-twentieth century, as well as for the flexible way the Church ultimately implemented this reform, as chapter 4 will show.

THREE INTEGRAL TASKS WITH A FOCUS ON CARE FOR THE NEEDY: ACTS 6:1–6

Perhaps the most remarkable New Testament account of the extension of apostolic ministry comes from the Acts of the Apostles 6:1–6. Shortly after being themselves filled with the Spirit at Pentecost (Acts 2:1–4), the apostles ("the Twelve") see a need, apparently for the distribution of food or of money from the common fund, that the apostles themselves are unable to fulfill effectively. The needy are widows described as Hellenists, which probably means that Greek was their primary language, no doubt a handicap within the largely Aramaic-speaking context of Jerusalem. The apostles ask the community to nominate seven men to care for these needs, and then commission the Seven by praying and laying hands on them. For a literal translation of the passage and an analysis of exegetical issues, see appendix 1.

A long and influential tradition of interpretation has understood this passage as describing the first commissioning, or even the first ordination, of deacons. The traditional understanding has been incorporated into ordination liturgies, and also has been used as a foundation story for the diaconate as a church office in many Christian denominations.[13] A careful study of this passage, however, shows that the author is not presenting the Seven as holders of the office of deacon as we will encounter it shortly in 1 Timothy 3:8–13 and in the writings of Ignatius and Polycarp. (See appendix 1 for the evidence.) To put it plainly: Acts 6:1–6 is not a foundation story, historical or legendary, for the diaconate. Nevertheless, the traditional interpretation uncovers another layer in the text, in which the Seven are models or types of what diaconal ministry should be. This typological reading has informed the Church's understanding of the diaconate from the earliest days. The consecratory prayer in the current Roman Catholic ordination rite uses this approach; without affirming that they actually *were* the first deacons, the prayer invokes their example for the ministry to which the candidate is being ordained.[14] Indeed, mention of the Seven as models for the diaconate, sometimes given in shorthand by an allusion to Stephen, is already found in third- and fourth-century ordination prayers for deacons.[15]

This kind of interpretation, at its simplest, finds qualities in the Seven, such as zeal, holiness, and good reputation, which seem particularly apt for deacons. But if we delve deeper into the text and also interpret it within its literary context in Acts, we uncover a perspective on ministry that is more specifically applicable to the diaconate. The ministry of the Seven is rooted in the mission of Christ and of the apostles and combines the three tasks of proclamation, prayer, and care for the needy, with a special focus on the last of these. In this the Seven provide a scripturally grounded model for the functional dimension of the diaconate, with its tasks of word, liturgy, and charity.

We see the three tasks combined in the ministry of the apostles as they move to extend their mission in the early chapters of Acts. They do so because the first followers of the resurrected Jesus, still centered in the temple precinct of Jerusalem, are becoming more numerous every day (Acts 2:41, 47; 5:14; 6:1). The community is growing through the power of the Spirit, which energizes the apostles' prayer (2:41–42 [including baptism], 47; 4:24–31), preaching (2:14–40; 3:12–26; 4:8–12), healings (3:1–10; 5:12–16), and care for the needy, a ministry handled through a common fund to which all are to contribute (2:44–45; 4:32–37).

When they commission the Seven, the Twelve at first sight appear to be giving away, or even splitting off, a distinct activity they cannot handle as the community grows. Thus, the Seven would have a single function: to take care of the Hellenist widows. And if they did this work effectively, there would be no reason to mention them further, as indeed we hear no more of the Seven as a group. But is this one limited function all that the Seven are given? The Twelve note that their own ministry incorporates three tasks (6:2–4): preaching and teaching the word, community prayer, and taking care of the needy. On closer inspection, the text shows that the apostles are bringing the Seven into all three tasks, albeit with a focus on an immediate requirement within the third one, and in a situation where the first two may be merely implicit at the outset.

The further development of the story points to this incorporation of the Seven into the full ministry of the Twelve. The only two of Seven about whom we learn anything further, Stephen and Philip, take on the broader apostolic mandate, especially teaching and preaching, but also performing healings. The narrative does not show Stephen, during the short time remaining before his martyrdom, engaged in community prayer, and Philip's reported role in prayer is limited to baptisms (8:12; 8:36–38). But the close way their overall ministry is modeled on that of the apostles expresses their full involvement extending the ministry of the Twelve. Of course, the specific activities of Stephen and Philip are at odds with the very narrow function given them at the original commissioning. Yet the narrative development points to a deeper reality about the three tasks: they constitute a unity in which each one points to the other. They have a mutually reinforcing inner logic. The proclamation of the good news invites the proclaimer to care in practical ways for human needs. Prayer is a response to evangelization and draws the pray-er into action on behalf of those who suffer. And so on. Indeed, this ministry of the Twelve is modeled on that of Jesus himself, whose mission in the world integrated teaching and proclamation, prayer, and a particular focus on those who suffer.

In bringing in the Seven to help with one of their tasks, then, the Twelve necessarily incorporate them into the whole apostolic ministry. The Seven enter that ministry through the third task, and therefore it will be useful to look more closely at how that task expresses and points to the others. Jesus is the model: he fed the hungry crowds, healed the sick, cast out demons, and shared his life with the marginalized. His actions aimed to alleviate real physical and emotional suffering, and at the same time to witness through signs to the inbreaking reality of God's kingdom. In Acts, the healings and works of mercy are also signs of the kingdom now spreading through the power of the Spirit. Because the Seven are commissioned as emissaries of the apostles to care for the Hellenist widows, then, this limited function carries within it the message of the good news and the power of the community's prayer.

From a careful reading of Acts 6:1–6 in its narrative context, the Seven emerge as fruitful models for diaconal ministry. The three tasks assigned to deacons, given in their shorthand form as word, liturgy, and charity, are fundamentally the same as those of the Twelve, which are preaching and proclamation, prayer, and care for the needy. The Seven are called into all three tasks with a focus on the third one. Chapters 4 through 6 will explore how the functional dimension of the diaconate is modeled on this incorporation into the apostolic ministry. The typological reading of Acts 6:1–6, then, by pointing to the functions of deacons and their place within the Church's ministries, actually offers a stronger and more specific scriptural grounding for the diaconate than would a simple foundation story, if that reading of the text could be supported.

OFFICE, RELATIONSHIP, AND EXAMPLE: 1 TIMOTHY 3:1–13

1 Timothy 3:1–13 includes the New Testament's only profile of deacons in office, and the passage does so in a way that seems strange to us, but would have been readily understandable to its original audience.[16] There is no explicit treatment of duties or functions, and no description of the church organization of which the deacons obviously are a part. Instead, the writer exhorts deacons to seek virtues (e.g., to be serious, self-controlled, good fathers and husbands) and to avoid vices (e.g., greed, insincerity, intemperance). This virtue and vice list follows a very similar list applied to an *episkopos*, a word best translated literally in our discussion here as "overseer" rather than "bishop," since the small community envisioned by 1 Timothy is not the kind of citywide diocese we associate with the title of bishop. For a literal translation of the text and an exegetical analysis underlying some of the conclusions presented here, see appendix 2.

The letter, whose identified author is Paul and whose addressee is his missionary colleague Timothy, offers exhortation and guidance for dealing with a crisis in teaching, moral conduct, and internal order within a Christian community located at Ephesus, a large city on what is today the western coast of Turkey.[17] The community's local leaders, specifically the overseer and deacons, have a key role in solving the crisis. We can point to three particular characteristics of the deacons that make them effective in this role: the kind of office they have in the Church; the relationships into which that office brings them; and their duty to be examples of the Christian life for others.

First, the deacons, like the overseer, hold a recognized church office, a stable ministry with multiple functions. Appendix 2 derives some of their tasks from a careful reading of 3:1–13. The deacons seem to assist the overseer in gathering the community and keeping order, as well as administering the community's funds. From comparison with other sources, it seems probable that the deacons also collected and distributed food (including the Eucharist).[18] The stability of their office is a result of their holding it for as long as elected or appointed to it.

An office of this kind differs from a charism, a gift of the Spirit, as we find these listed at 1 Corinthians 12:4–31, Romans 12:6–7, and Ephesians 4:11. Those with charisms include, for example, teachers, prophets, evangelists, speakers in tongues, and healers; the lists in these three letters differ from each other and obviously are illustrative, not precise or exhaustive. The passages stress the generosity of the Spirit, and do not aim to provide directives for Church organization or governance. The distinction between office and charism, and the relations between them, have been the source of considerable contention among both New Testament scholars and Christians of different denominations seeking to support particular kinds of Church order.[19] In looking at these letters alongside 1 Timothy 3:1–3, however, a basic difference does emerge, even if there may have been overlap in details. An office is a stable ministry, with multiple functions, held through some kind of election or appointment. Those with spiritual gifts, however, seem to be put forward by the community as and when needed, as vehicles of a single outstanding function, such as prophecy or teaching.[20] This does not mean that the overseer and deacons could not or did not exercise particular spiritual gifts (the overseer in 1 Tim 3:2, for example, should be "apt at teaching") or that as Church officers they were necessarily in competition with charismatic ministers.[21] Exercised rightly, an office supports and may be a vehicle for the exercise of various spiritual gifts in the community, but the office itself is not identified with one of those gifts. This understanding of the diaconate as office clarifies the tasks of diaconal ministry even today: the diaconate does not and need not (as one sometimes hears) "have a charism," but deacons should encourage, inspire, and at times be a vehicle for the various gifts and talents through which the Spirit works in the Church.[22]

Second, the diaconate that emerges from this text is strongly relational. Although the overseer and the deacons obviously have distinct responsibilities, the structure of the passage, with its parallelism and word repetitions, puts much more emphasis on the strong relation between the two offices than on their differences. (Reading the text in appendix 2 is enough to make this clear.) The rhetorical parallelism expresses how they work together, under the overseer's direction, for a common goal: to promote true belief and right conduct in a community riven by conflict. The need for a definite relationship under the overseer's guidance flows from the fact that these offices require a specific collaboration in tasks, rather than (as in the case of the spiritual gifts) a more general ordering to the upbuilding of the Church, envisioned as a body with different members.[23] As presented in 1 Timothy, moreover, the relation between overseer and deacons is part of a broader set of relationships that must function well for true faith and good conduct to flourish in the Church. These local leaders serve Christ by serving the Apostle Paul and his delegate Timothy, and they also serve the community for which they are called to minister.[24]

A final dimension of diaconal ministry presented in 1 Timothy 3:8-13 is its capacity, and indeed calling, to be an example for the community. This is expressed in the virtue and vice lists by which the passage is structured. The stable, multifunctional character of these offices makes it both possible and critically important for the holders of them to exemplify certain broadly applicable qualities for the community. Accordingly, the virtues the overseer and deacons are exhorted to practice are important both for the right exercise of the offices themselves and for the Christian life generally: sound faith, self-control, truthfulness, seriousness of purpose; avoiding intemperance, greed, gossip or slander, and so on. In 1 Timothy, in fact, the need to exemplify the Christian life for others runs through the whole letter. Paul the apostle and author presents himself as a model of conversion (1:12–17) and exhorts his delegate Timothy to be an example of unshakeable faith (1:18–19a; 6:11–14; and esp. 4:12). The overseer and deacons have a similar role in modeling the virtues of the Christian life for the community, whose constituent groups are urged to exemplify particular virtues with special clarity (2:8–15; 5:3–20; 6:1–2, 11–19).[25] All, but especially those with the visibility of responsible positions, are exhorted to be models of the Christian life to others. For the community of 1 Timothy, the virtues to be modeled include those both of right belief and good conduct. This does not mean the deacons must be perfect paragons of faith and virtue; the letter would not be exhorting them at such length if they did not need correction.[26] But because they hold a stable, multifunctional office, strongly bound both to the leader of the local church and to the community, the Church depends on them to be examples, so far as their fallen natures allow, of the life of Christian faith.

A DIACONATE PATTERNED ON CHRIST THE SERVANT: IGNATIUS AND POLYCARP

The idea of the deacon as an example of faith and conduct found in 1 Timothy is carried a step further by two of the earliest Church fathers, Ignatius and Polycarp. Both were leaders of local communities; at this stage the lineage to future bishops is more secure, so we may translate their title *episkopos* as "bishop." Ignatius, on his way to martyrdom in Rome, wrote a series of letters to Christian communities (six letters survive) as well as one letter to Polycarp. These documents cover a range of doctrinal and Church order concerns; exhortations to follow the bishop, who is assisted by elders/presbyters and deacons, are a recurrent theme. Polycarp's only surviving text is the letter addressed to the same community at Philippi in present-day Greece to whom Paul had written earlier.[27]

Polycarp's letter is an exhortation to right belief and upstanding conduct with many similarities to 1 Timothy. The distinctive element here is that the deacons in their virtues are called on to model Christ. The treatment of deacons involves a virtue and vice list like that in 1 Timothy.[28] There is no close pairing between the diaconate and any other office, as we find in the pairing of overseer and deacons in 1 Timothy, and no mention of a bishop anywhere in Polycarp's letter. The list begins by exhorting them to be "servants/deacons [*diakonoi*] of God and Christ and not of people," and ends by urging them to "walk according to the truth of the Lord, who was the servant/deacon [*diakonos*] of all." Thus, Polycarp bookends the virtue and vice list with the themes of "the deacon as servant" and "Christ the model."[29] At Vatican II, *Lumen Gentium* would use this quote from Polycarp as the key to diaconal identity, as we will see in chapter 5.

The particular way in which deacons model Christ as servants is somewhat more clearly expressed by Ignatius, who places a dominant stress on the leadership role of a bishop and places deacons together with elders/presbyters in a tripartite ministry, "appointed according to the mind of Jesus Christ who set them up firmly according to his own will, so that through his Holy Spirit they would not waver."[30] In this context the bishop presides as God the Father, the presbyters-elders make up a council like that of the apostles, and the deacons are exhorted to be like Christ.[31] This set of similes implies that deacons model Christ by being subject to the bishop as Christ was obedient to the Father. But Ignatius nowhere says so explicitly, noting only that all the faithful should be subject to the bishop in this way.[32] Ignatius does exhort the deacons to be servants of God's Church.[33]

Both Ignatius and Polycarp are writing letters of exhortation, and for expressive purposes they pile up similes and metaphors without much definition or precision. They do, however, insist that deacons in particular should model Christ in some way that has to do with serving the Church and the faithful.

Neither bishops nor presbyters/elders are exhorted to represent Christ: this theme is distinctive for deacons. This typology of Christ for the deacon found its way into some of the ancient ordination prayers, and is the culminating image in the consecratory prayer of the current Roman Catholic Rite.[34] The proponents of a modern diaconate, moreover, built upon and significantly extended this insight in developing the vision of the deacon as icon of Christ the servant.

Several themes that are foundational for understanding diaconal identity have emerged from this chapter's engagement with key texts from the New Testament, Ignatius, and Polycarp. The New Testament overall shows the early Christian communities developing a diversity of ministries in response to missionary and pastoral needs, providing a pattern for the development of a diaconal ministry addressing modern conditions, but also rooted in the early Church. Acts 6:1–6, though not an account of the first ordination of deacons, yields a pattern for diaconal ministry incorporating the three interrelated tasks of word and proclamation, liturgy and prayer, and charity and care of the needy, with an emphasis on the third task. The diaconate appears in 1 Timothy as a stable ministry of assistance within the local Church leadership, with a strongly collaborative relation to the head of the community. As the holder of a recognized office, the deacon is called upon to be a visible example of the Christian life. This exemplifying role is further developed by Ignatius and Polycarp, who present the deacon as a model of Christ the servant, in language that is suggestive if not precise. All of these themes are picked up and developed as the diaconate is shaped during its formative history, to which we now turn.

CHAPTER THREE

• • • • • •

ENVISIONING THE DIACONATE BEFORE THE COUNCIL

Our two complementary models of diaconal identity, Christ the servant and minister of the threshold, are rooted in the movement to revive the diaconate that gathered strength after 1945, and that ultimately brought this idea to the Second Vatican Council in 1962. By the middle of the twentieth century, diaconal office had existed in the Western Church only as a transitional stage on the road to priesthood, rather than as an independent ministry, for over a thousand years. The history that led to this situation is beyond the scope of this book; our story begins here, with the modern proposal for permanent diaconal ministry. The pastoral and missionary challenges of the time gave the impetus to that proposal, which was drawn to the diaconate by possibilities inherent in this fossil of an ancient office. Although there was no actual diaconate on which to reflect until after the council, the proponents were able to imagine the major contours of the revived office in ways that shaped the council's deliberations and still contribute to our understanding of diaconal identity today.

ANOMALIES IN THE STATUS QUO IN THE MID-TWENTIETH CENTURY

Although almost completely unquestioned for centuries, the situation of the diaconal office, understood as merely a stage in ecclesiastical advancement, was in certain respects anomalous. This caught the attention of some theologians and Church leaders as they grappled with the Church's challenges in their own time. The anomalies—historical, sacramental, and ecumenical—encouraged them to explore a revival of the diaconate as one way to address those needs.

First, the status quo for the diaconate could seem odd because, as we saw in the last chapter, it had not always been so and indeed was not so in the first centuries of the Church. An alternative was there in the historical record, and in the writings of the New Testament and the Church fathers. Even before the historians specially focused on the diaconate did their research in the 1940s and 1950s, a vast scholarship on Church history had been building up since the nineteenth century, demonstrating patterns of change and development in the past, and suggesting models for reform.

Second, the status quo for the diaconate was anomalous within the sacrament of holy orders. In this matter the Council of Trent (1545–63) suggested lines of inquiry without providing any clear direction. This sixteenth-century council was convened to define and reassert Catholic doctrine against Protestantism, and to introduce reforms into the Roman Catholic Church. Trent confirmed that the deacon is a member of the ordained clergy but left it ambiguous whether he belongs to the major orders, with priests and bishops, or to the minor ones.[1]

The conciliar document notes that "the functions of Holy Orders from deacon to doorkeeper have been received with praise in the church since apostolic times....Hence the Holy Council, desiring to restore the earliest practice, decrees that from now on these ministries are to be performed only by those constituted in the said orders."[2] Some activists for the diaconate in the twentieth century would interpret this formulation as a directive to revive the ancient office of deacon, presumably on the grounds that, in practice, the diaconal functions could never be carried out by transitional deacons only. But that is hardly the point. The real thrust at Trent is to defend holy orders in their full range (including the minor orders) against Protestant criticisms of their sacramentality. The council texts moreover envision the diaconate in the transitional form that was accepted practice in the Western Church from earlier times.[3]

Trent's ambiguity about whether the diaconate was a major or minor grade within holy orders was clarified in Pius XII's 1947 apostolic constitution *Sacramentum Ordinis*.[4] This document was not primarily concerned with the diaconate: the goal was to define the effective means (matter and form) in the sacrament of holy orders. Since the pope covered the ordination of bishops, priests, and deacons (and not any of the minor orders), his treatment strongly implied, if it did not explicitly affirm, that the diaconate participated in the major orders along with priests and bishops. This is where things stood on the eve of the council. Yet grouped in this tripartite sacramental ministry, the diaconate was in the anomalous position of having no ministerial function or purpose.

Finally, the status quo for the diaconate in the Western Church was anomalous from an ecumenical perspective, and even to a degree within the Roman Catholic communion itself. Deacons, who could be married, had continued to hold a permanent and recognized office in the Orthodox churches, in generally unbroken tradition from apostolic times. When, in the centuries after the Crusades, some of those churches came into communion with Rome, they normally kept their ecclesiastical traditions, including a "permanent" diaconate allowing marriage. These Eastern Catholic churches (Ukrainian, Antiochene, Coptic, Melkite, and the rest), all based in Eastern Europe or in the Middle East, were full members of the Roman Catholic Church. As in most of the Orthodox churches, the diaconate in these Eastern Catholic churches had a significant role in the divine liturgy (Eucharist), but little independent ministerial identity beyond this. In many of the Eastern Catholic churches, moreover, the diaconate had fallen into disuse under the pressure to conform with Western practice. Nevertheless, the existence of a living ministry for deacons among the Orthodox, and even within a corner of the Roman Catholic Church, suggested for the Western Church the question, "Why not here?"[5]

This question presented itself even more starkly when the Roman Catholic diaconate was compared with diaconates in some Protestant denominations that, since the Reformation, had developed an office for deacons (and deaconesses) as a recognized ministry, mainly in the areas of church administration and care of the needy.[6] The comparison between Catholic and Protestant diaconates was particularly striking in Germany, where Protestants and Catholics lived side by side and developed institutions that were in certain respects parallel. In the nineteenth century, there developed in the Protestant churches communities of deaconesses and (in smaller numbers) of "brothers" who were often referred to as "deacons." The women and some of the men remained unmarried while living in community and engaged in their work, which was focused on the sick, the indigent, and marginalized.[7] While their style of life was modeled to some degree on the active Catholic religious orders of both women and men who were involved in many of the same activities, the Protestants understood this care of the needy in light of the traditional reading of Acts 6:1–6 as recounting the commissioning of deacons for the care of the needy.

Indeed, what in a Catholic context was understood as charity or the corporal works of mercy, the German Protestants came to call *Diakonie*, giving the general Greek term *diakonia* (meaning ministry, service, or acting on behalf of another person) the specific sense of Christian social work, functionally distinct from witness/proclamation/preaching on the one hand, and from parish and community life on the other.[8] By the twentieth century, both the Catholic and Protestant churches had developed large social service and relief organizations involved in *Diakonie*. On the Protestant side, the workers could be called deacons and deaconesses. But for Catholics, this characterization was off limits: "deacon" was merely a transitional step on the road to priesthood, defined by liturgical rather than pastoral or charitable functions. In Germany, then, the anomaly of the Catholic status quo was that deacons had no special focus on *Diakonie*, as this word was generally understood; whereas Catholics doing *Diakonie* could not be deacons.

In hindsight it is easy to point out these anomalies—historical, sacramental, and ecumenical—but none of them was likely to take on any importance beyond mentions here and there in theological articles or the Catholic press unless conditions on the ground drew attention to them. Even then, a millennium of settled practice, together with widely held views about ministry and the Church that supported that practice, had a weight of authority that would make any move to revive the diaconate as a permanent ministry controversial.

PASTORAL AND MISSIONARY NEEDS

The impetus for a new permanent diaconate open to married men came from three independent directions, more or less simultaneously, in the late 1940s. Within a few years the activists from the different sides would coalesce into a movement.[9]

One strand grew out of the German branch of Caritas, the Catholic social service agency based in Lucerne, Switzerland. Already in the 1930s, groups of professional social workers had organized themselves into groups, seeking a life of prayer and formation that would strengthen their commitment to serving refugees, the poor, and the sick. The massive human suffering caused by two world wars and an economic depression, particularly in Germany and Austria, gave special urgency to the work, and to the Church's role in sponsoring that work. Focused mainly on the vocation to charitable service and envisioning deacons as permanently employed in that activity, these groups found their most eloquent spokesman in Hannes Kramer, a professional social worker who was active in Southern Germany.[10] The understanding of this work as *Diakonie*, as well as the model of Protestant deacons and deaconesses professionally dedicated to it, made it natural for the Caritas groups to form these "diaconate circles."

A second impetus, also from Germany, responded to the disruptions of parish life caused by Nazism and war. In 1936, the Nazi regime sent Joseph Hornef, a judge, into internal exile in the Protestant region of Upper Hesse, where he remained with his family until after the war. Disheartened by the lack of any organized Catholic life, Hornef became a de facto pastoral assistant at the nearby mission church that was attached to a faraway parish. At the Dachau concentration camp in Bavaria, meanwhile, the camp administration separated the clergy into a section of the prison cut off from the other internees, with the purpose of keeping them from exercising any pastoral ministry. While interned in the "priests' block" there, Otto Pies and Wilhelm Schamoni reflected together on how, in the absence of priests, committed laymen might lead prayer services, preach, provide instruction in the faith, and distribute communion. As in Hornef's case, the question was how the Church could continue to function sacramentally and pastorally in the absence of priests. For both situations, a revival of the diaconate offered the possibility of bringing the strength and permanence of ordained clergy to address these pastoral crises. After the war, Pies published an account of their experience and reflections about ministry while at Dachau.[11] The image of priests imprisoned apart from the faithful offered a compelling story in a world where, in fact, there was a shortage of priests almost everywhere except in the United States and a few countries of Western Europe. The shortage was particularly acute in the large regions of the world where Catholics were lightly planted or in the minority, but even in places with large Catholic populations, many priests were overburdened with a combination of sacramental, pastoral, and administrative tasks. By the late 1940s, Hornef and Schamoni had become tireless campaigners for a permanent diaconate. For them, the immediate problem was a shortage of priests. They saw deacons as being employed mainly in secular occupations and assisting parish priests on a part-time basis with liturgy, catechesis, and various pastoral tasks.[12]

The third springboard for the diaconate movement was provided by the churches outside Europe and North America. Many of these regions could be described as still in the mission stage of development. The shortage of priests often was truly severe, and in some places a cadre of lay missionaries and teachers was already assisting them in important ways. The idea of ordaining some of these laypeople to a recognized ministry probably originated from the proposals for a permanent diaconate in Europe, but the representatives of the missionary churches quickly added their unique perspective.[13] The possibility of empowering lay catechists to distribute communion (at that time a function reserved to priests), to act as ordinary ministers of baptism, and to celebrate marriage proved appealing to some Church leaders in Latin America, Africa, and Asia. Such ministers also could be strengthened further in their catechetical role through some kind of formation.

By the early 1950s, activists from each of these three directions had come to know each other through their published articles, which appeared both in scholarly journals and in the Catholic press. At this point, a group of theologians came on the scene to give the different viewpoints some intellectual structure. Karl Rahner, then at the University of Innsbruck, was particularly influenced by Hannes Kramer, and provided the most important theological support to the project, both before and during the council. Paul Winninger of the University of Strasbourg worked more closely with Hornef and provided an important bridge to the French-speaking world.[14] Several bishops and leaders in missionary orders began to offer support for the revived diaconate in Africa, Asia, and Latin America through writings and at conferences during the course of the 1950s.[15]

Each of the three pastoral and missionary situations that contributed to the movement had a distinct functional emphasis. By integrating these functions into a single proposal, the activists had one rationale for imagining the revival of diaconal office as the solution. The Caritas context stressed charitable work; those responding to a shortage of priests emphasized liturgical and pastoral roles; while the "new Church" or "missionary" perspective sprang from catechesis and extended into enlarged pastoral and sacramental ministries. Together they incorporated what became the three tasks of word, liturgy, and charity that Vatican II later formulated for deacons, tasks we have already seen as integral to the apostolic ministry in Acts. The confluence of these three practical situations into the same theological and pastoral conversation in the 1950s was a factor in pointing toward a revival of the diaconate. Any one of these pastoral or missionary needs, considered in isolation, might rather have suggested the development or expansion of a religious order or a lay organization. But taken together, they pointed to diaconal office with its multiple interrelated functions; and they suggested a way to overcome the anomalies of the status quo.[16]

The activists of the 1950s had well-considered reasons, then, both theological and pastoral, for proposing the revival of the diaconate as a permanent ministry. But their proposal would alter a millennium of settled practice, and that was unlikely to happen without some encouragement from the highest levels of the Church.

SIGNALS FROM ROME

In the decade after World War II, an increasing number of articles promoting a revived diaconate appeared in the European Catholic press and in scholarly journals, but the idea did not yet attract enough attention to spark criticism or debate. Two events emanating from Rome changed this dynamic, making the revival of the diaconate start to look like a real possibility, and thereby drawing out some determined opposition. In 1957, the founder of the Missionary Brothers of the Countryside proposed a revival of the diaconate, with celibacy, suitable for brothers living under religious vows or seminarians with an authentic vocation to serve the Church but not prepared to meet the intellectual challenge of seminary studies.[17] The author sent the article to Pope Pius XII, who in turn forwarded it to the Holy Office (the successor of the Holy Roman Inquisition, and forerunner of the Congregation for the Doctrine of the Faith) "for study." Later that year, at the second annual Conference on the Apostolate of the Laity, the pope remarked, "We know that some are currently thinking about introducing an order for the diaconate understood as an ecclesiastical function independent of the priesthood. The idea, today at least, is not yet ripe."[18] Skeptics of the new idea might consider that this pronouncement closed the matter, but supporters pounced on the "not yet" and began to ask in a more pointed way what conditions would make the idea opportune. The pace of publications supporting a revived diaconate picked up markedly.

The Holy Office, while cool to the idea of a permanent diaconate, was treating the overall question as still open to debate. But the Office seems to have considered the more radical proposal for a diaconate open to married men to be outside the legitimate bounds of theological discussion. In 1958, the censors of the Office refused Winninger permission to publish the monograph *Toward a Renewal of the Diaconate* until he cut out any positive consideration of married deacons.[19]

The second event emanating from Rome proved decisive in sparking a serious debate about the diaconate, and of course later culminated in its implementation. This event was Pope St. John XXIII's announcement in 1959 that he would call an ecumenical council. The activists and theologians supporting the new diaconate saw an opening. The pace of publications accelerated further as they raced to get on the council's agenda. By 1962, when the council convened, Karl Rahner and Herbert Vorgrimler had edited and published *Diaconia in Christo*: weighing in at over six hundred pages, and including a comprehensive bibliography that by itself implied that the idea was "ripe" for serious consideration, the anthology offered contributions from leading scholars on the history and theology of the diaconate together with reports from around the world explaining how deacons might address varying pastoral needs.[20] Nevertheless, in light of the signals from Rome—particularly the alarm at any idea of a married diaconate—the activists could not be confident that the coming council would adopt their proposal, or even that it would get on the agenda.

FOR AND AGAINST

Particularly once the prospect of an ecumenical council turned the new diaconate into a practical possibility, skeptics began to study the question more deeply and to make objections.

By the time the full council debated the diaconate question, in 1963 and 1964, the arguments of both sides had been digested and could be developed by the council participants. If we give the preconcilar debate a careful hearing, it becomes clear that much more was at stake than an institutional readjustment. Each side was committed to a quite different view of the clergy, and of the Church itself.[21]

The opponents of the proposed diaconate appealed to widely held and influential views that virtually identified ordained ministry with priesthood—with the "power" to say Mass and hear confessions. Priests, in turn, were understood to have a special, semimonastic call to holiness that included celibacy. This priestly self-understanding, moreover, stood at a high-water mark in the 1950s. From such a perspective, miscellaneous "apostolates" performed by married men could hardly merit ordination. Indeed, they would tempt the Church to lose its Eucharistic focus. Moreover, any move to open the clergy to married men would drain recruits from the priesthood and undermine the commitment to celibacy among priests.[22]

The proposed diaconate also ran afoul of a generally juridical and institutional view of the Church that stressed clearly defined roles, uniform administration, and a cautious attitude toward innovation. Some of the proponents had suggested that married deacons living in nonchurch settings would be a kind of bridge between the higher clergy and the laity. To the opponents, such a bridge function looked useless and confusing, blurring the distinct missions given to clergy and laity. As for any bridge function between the clergy and the secular world, that was precisely the role assigned to a faithful layperson. Moreover, in the opponents' view, nothing in the contemporary situation justified a departure from the centuries-old practice of a transitional diaconate: a more effective and less disruptive solution would be to address current needs by strengthening existing lay organizations or offering to lay ministers various forms of public commissioning that stopped short of ordination. The Church could also extend and strengthen the lay apostolates directed by priests and known as Catholic Action, which already were active in many regions. Ordaining married men risked "decapitating" these apostolates by draining them of their lay leaders. In general, the opponents stressed the newness of the proposal and the many problems that could be foreseen in forming deacons and supervising their ministry.

The juridical model of the Church and the priestly view of ministry had filled the seminary textbooks for generations. These ideas can be called conservative both because they emphasize institutional continuity and because by the 1950s they had, for many Church leaders, the force of what jurists call "settled law." Such views also enjoyed wide support in the Roman curia among men such as Cardinal Alfredo Ottaviani, Secretary of the Holy Office, who would lead opposition to the diaconate at the council.

By contrast, the idea of reviving the diaconate had found a congenial reception in currents of theology and pastoral practice that had been gaining momentum in West Germany, France, and the Low Countries since the interwar years.[23] This region, particularly West Germany and to a lesser extent France, faced a pastoral crisis due to the shortage of priests, and the German activists had patterned the proposed diaconate on their own social workers and pastoral volunteers.[24] The diaconate also fit into a variety of theological movements that can be called "reformist" in the sense that they elaborated a vision of Church and ministry that claimed to be more grounded in Scripture, and more adapted to contemporary needs, than the juridical model. In general, this reform impulse was more optimistic about change, and the proponents saw the opportunity to overcome the anomalies of the diaconate—historical, sacramental, and ecumenical—in the current status quo.

For the proponents, the developing view of the Church as "communion," expressed through images such as the Body of Christ and the people of God, tended to diminish the juridical stress on sharply defined roles, to loosen the strict focus on the priestly character of the clergy, and to allow for a broader emphasis on ministers as servants of the community.[25] While not putting priestly celibacy into question, they could see positive dimensions to a married diaconate, whether sacramentally expressing Christ's marriage to the Church, or putting forth a distinctly ecclesial image of married men in regions where husbands were staying away and leaving the churchgoing to their wives. The reformers also envisioned a Church that would be less authoritarian and more like Christ the servant who gave himself for all. For these theologians and bishops, deacons would act as a vanguard within the clergy itself for this reforming vision of the Church.

Besides stressing the pastoral need for deacons to extend and support the ministry of priests, the proponents argued that there were faithful laymen who were performing diaconal functions already—"anonymous deacons," in Rahner's phrase—and that the Church should strengthen their ministry by using its treasury of sacramental grace.[26] The definition or listing of these functions varied widely. As to what made them diaconal, the proponents offered few specifics. The functions envisioned could include care for the needy, pastoral care and administration, catechesis, sacramental and liturgical roles, or leading community prayer, with different emphases depending on the writer's interest and the needs identified. The opponents, of course, saw no reason that these functions, separately or together, should be part of an ordained ministry, except where already carried out by priests.

IMAGINING MINISTERIAL IDENTITY

As they prepared for the council, the theologians and activists sought to imagine what the office of deacon would be like if it became a permanent ministry. But without an actual modern diaconate to reflect on, they could hardly be definitive about who these deacons would be and what the Church would task them to do. The practical contexts that gave rise to the proposal envisioned a variety of real-life settings: that of a social and relief worker; or an assistant extending the work of pastors in community life; or a catechist in a missionary context, holding together local church life when priests were rarely present. No one could say for sure if deacons would be full-time employees of the church or of a church-related organization, or whether they would earn a living in a nonchurch job and act function-ally as volunteers.

In a general way the proponents all assume that the diac-onate is about service. Often, particularly in the German lan-guage writers, this seems to refer particularly to *Diakonie* in the standard understanding of that term as taking care of the needy, although some combination of catechesis, altar service, and leading the community in prayer outside the Mass are often assumed as well, if not always spelled out explicitly. The stress on service, besides being rooted in a translation of *diakonos*, obviously is meant to exclude priestly roles like eucharistic pre-siding and hearing confessions. This service focus would give deacons a potential place and functional role in the clergy, one that is distinct from priesthood.

Though the idea of diaconal service could not be defined concretely without a ministry on the ground, the broad accep-tance among proponents of service as the defining characteristic of the diaconate proved to be decisive in the later development of a diaconal identity modeled on Christ the servant. Those sup-porting a revived diaconate saw service, including especially care of the needy, as part of the apostolic ministry that the clergy was called to exercise.[27]

In this view, having ministers dedicated to service who are integral to the tripartite clergy with bishops and priests would make the clergy itself more fully apostolic and would help to strengthen the whole mission of the Church. Opponents of the diaconate proposal, for their part, understood the clergy's role in terms of governance and sacramental powers. Both the clergy and the laity were called to service in the sense of the corporal works of mercy, of course, but precisely for this reason the oppo-nents saw no reason to incorporate a distinct service ministry into the clergy. This broader debate about the clergy and the Church was taken up by the council and provided the context for the way in which the council documents sketched a vision of diaconal identity based on service, as we will see in the next chapter.

In imagining deacons for the contemporary world, some activists and theologians highlighted an important "bridge" role between the higher clergy and the laity, or between the Church and the world.[28] This role had several dimensions and possibilities, but in all of them the deacon would be a member of the clergy "tied to the altar" through liturgical functions, but also someone who lives and perhaps is also typically employed in a nonchurch setting. In this context, the deacon is seen as moving out from the Eucharist and from the Church at prayer into a broader social space, whether this was inhabited by the lay faithful or by a non-Catholic, non-Christian, and even militantly anti-Christian world.[29] At the very least, the deacon was imagined living outside the rectory or religious house, usually married and often with a family, and thus closer to the experience of the lay faithful. If deacons were to work primarily in nonchurch jobs, this would make them, in a social and economic sense, yet more like the laity, and often place them normally in explicitly nonreligious settings. Even those proponents who assumed deacons would be employed in church-affiliated organizations imagined them typically involved in social or relief work in which they would encounter the suffering and marginalized of the wider world, or on mission in places where priests were rarely seen. This outward movement from the altar to a broader Catholic community and to the world at large, which the activists and theologians imagined before the council, is the kernel for understanding the deacon as minister of the threshold.

The council would offer the opportunity to air this debate about the diaconate, to explore compromises between opposing views, and to decide whether the diaconate, in some form, should be revived for the twentieth-century Church.

CHAPTER FOUR

• • • • • •

VATICAN II

Reform, Continuity, and Caution

Two brief passages within the voluminous documents of the
Second Vatican Council (1962–65) provide a basic charter for
the modern diaconate and sketch a ministerial identity for
deacons modeled on Christ the servant. The idea of reviving
diaconal ministry entered the council as part of its debate
about the Church; the key text for the diaconate is Section 29
of the Dogmatic Constitution on the Church *Lumen Gentium*
(November 21, 1964). Section 16 of the Decree on Missionary
Activity *Ad Gentes*, adopted a year later on December 7, 1965,
places the diaconate envisioned in *Lumen Gentium* into a
mission context, adding some important dimensions.[1]

Though not one of the major questions discussed by the
council, the diaconate generated a broad and heated debate,
both on the council floor and in the drafting committees. The
issues, which had already emerged in the council's preparatory
phases, came to a head in the debate about the evolving text of
Lumen Gentium during the council's second session, in the fall
of 1963. The final treatment of the diaconate in Section 29 bears
the marks of compromise between different viewpoints and,
more broadly, of the attempt to reconcile the call for renewal
and change with a commitment to continuity in the Church's
tradition and practice.

Both *Lumen Gentium* 29 and *Ad Gentes* 16 are part of the body of council documents, and accordingly must be interpreted, not only in the terms of the debates behind specific provisions, but in light of the structure, style, and broader themes of those documents. We will therefore consider the significance of the council for the diaconate in two steps. This chapter shows how the underlying debates and compromises influenced the content of *Lumen Gentium* 29. The next chapter provides a close reading of this text, along with *Ad Gentes* 16, uncovering the foundations for a diaconal identity modeled not just on service in general, but specifically on Christ the servant.[2]

A NEW FRAMEWORK FOR THE DEBATE

Vatican II was an ecumenical council (meaning one that brings together leaders of the Catholic Church in the whole world), the twenty-first in the history of the Church, according to the standard reckoning. As such, the council assembled bishops, patriarchs, and heads of male religious orders from all over the globe, generally gathering 2,250–2,500 voting members in its plenary sessions over four years. This gathering provided a new and enhanced framework for the debate about the diaconate, incorporating a far broader representation and one with a fully international perspective compared with the mainly Europe-based conversation up to this time. The strong and coordinated support of Latin American bishops for the diaconate, and to a lesser degree those from Africa and Asia, would give new weight to the proposal. The opposition, though smaller in numbers than the proponents, would spread well beyond the Roman curia and a few European theologians to include a broadly international group.[3]

In addition, because an ecumenical council offered the practical possibility of carrying the day for the diaconate proposal over the objections so far voiced by the Holy Office, the speeches in the council generally have a practical and deliberative character that differs from preconcilar writings, which were more exploratory and theological. Supporters of the renewed diaconate at the council tend to avoid appeals to ideas that might be controversial, to minimize the scope of innovation in their proposal, to seek compromise and common ground, and to highlight the expected positive results. Opponents give a greater stress to practical risks and problems, while continuing to argue that the innovation is unnecessary and doctrinally incoherent. This practical orientation, besides its usefulness as persuasion, also fitted the background and interests of the speakers, most of whom were bishops with pastoral responsibilities, rather than trained theologians.

The two phases of preparation for the council during 1960 and 1961, called Ante-preparatory and Preparatory, reveal undercurrents that would come to the surface during the council debates.[4] First, there was widespread support for the diaconate among prospective council participants based on pastoral and missionary needs, but opposition by Cardinal Ottaviani and other members of the Preparatory Theological Commission, charged with overseeing the drafting of documents, would provide a powerful counterbalance. Second, the idea of clergy not bound to celibacy was perhaps the most alarming component of the diaconate proposal among skeptics. Third, the possibility was floated of implementing the new diaconate only in selected regions, with or without celibacy, depending on regional pastoral needs. The decisions about such selective implementation would involve the pope, and, potentially, regional bishops' conferences. This was a way of softening opposition, although for those who believed it was simply a bad idea to make the diaconate a permanent ministry, such uneven implementation would merely add an element of confusion to a fundamentally misguided change.

By the spring of 1962, it was clear that the diaconate proposal would become part of the council's debate only if it were included in a major document on the Church.[5] The Preparatory Theological Commission was charged with producing a draft on this subject for the first session of the council, which would open in October 1962. It was no surprise that the draft document "On the Church," distributed in the summer of 1962 to those invited to attend the first session in the fall, was silent on the matter.[6]

However, two directives that John XXIII gave to the participants in his opening address, *Gaudet Mater Ecclesia* (October
11, 1962), gave a shape to the council deliberations that would
prove helpful to the proponents of reviving the diaconate.[7] First,
the pope stated that the council's goal would not be to restate
doctrine or to condemn errors, but to express the deposit of faith
in a way that would speak most effectively to the contemporary world. This goal tended to encourage ideas that promised to
strengthen the Church's missionary and pastoral outreach, provided that those ideas remained in harmony with the deposit of
faith and with tradition. The supporters of reviving the diaconate would make just such a case for their proposal.

Second, the pope's address called on the council to promote
Christian unity, a goal that was further emphasized by the presence of invited guests representing Orthodox, Anglican, and
Protestant denominations at all the plenary sessions. This gave
the council an ecumenical orientation (in the common use of
"ecumenical," as including all Christians). Both the goal set forth
by the pope and the presence of the observers encouraged the
participants to give consideration to ideas and practices found
among the "separated brethren," provided (again) that such
ideas or practices were in harmony with the deposit of faith and
with Catholic tradition. Proponents of reviving the diaconate as
a permanent ministry for married men could, and would, point
to an unbroken tradition in the Orthodox churches (and also,
to some extent, in the Eastern Catholic churches in communion
with Rome) as a counterweight to the millennium-old practice
of a solely transitional diaconate in the Western Church. The
Protestant diaconates focused on church administration and
care of the needy had already influenced the way Catholic activists envisioned a revived diaconate, particularly in Germany, as
we have seen. However, probably because the Protestant office
lacked the sacramental basis that is central to any Catholic
understanding of the diaconate, speakers at the council did not
appeal to Protestant practice as a model.

THE DEBATE IN THE COUNCIL

In the council's first session, the Preparatory Theological Commission's initial draft document on the Church, which had passed over the diaconate in silence, was remanded to committee for substantial revisions. This opened up the possibility of a positive treatment in the next round of drafting. During the winter of 1962–63, several informal working groups produced new versions of "On the Church," which they hoped the Doctrinal Commission, successor to the Preparatory Theological Commission, would adopt and present at the council's second session, in the fall of 1963.[8] During the early winter, Karl Rahner mailed copies of *Diaconia in Christo* to all the members of the Doctrinal Commission. He also distributed, more widely, a Latin translation of the table of contents, so that council participants who could not read German at least would get an idea of the volume's impressive range of documentation.[9] Meanwhile, among the different versions of "On the Church," the draft of Monsignor Gérard Philips, a Belgian priest who was serving as a consultant to the Doctrinal Commission, was adopted as the next draft to be presented to the full council. The Philips document included a brief proposal in favor of the diaconate, finally placing the question on the council's agenda.

From October 4 to 16, 1963, the council debated chapter 2 of the Philips document "On the Church," covering bishops, priests, and deacons. This section included the diaconate language, but the really explosive question raised by the full chapter was "collegiality." This word refers to a cluster of ideas that may be simplified, for our purposes at any rate, to the doctrine that the bishops as a body (or "college") govern the Church in communion with the pope. Opponents of collegiality saw in it a weakening of papal sovereignty that would destroy the unity of the Church and undermine the explicit teaching of Vatican I's *Pastor Aeternus*, the dogmatic constitution that defined papal infallibility.[10] The joining of these two controversial issues, collegiality and the diaconate, probably contributed to a hardening of positions on both of them.

43

The Philips document "On the Church" aimed at compromise. His language was cautious and diplomatic, sometimes to the point of studied ambiguity, and the short section on the diaconate was characteristic. It begins by placing deacons within the hierarchy "at a lower rank than bishops and priests." The deacon has some limited liturgical functions: to serve at Mass, to act as an "extraordinary minister of baptism," and to distribute communion. He undertakes such charitable and administrative tasks as may be assigned by the competent authorities. But noting that the current practice is not and has not been universal, the document suggests that

> in the future it will be possible for the diaconate to be exercised as a special and permanent rank of the hierarchy, where the Church shall decide this to be useful for pastoral reasons; and this may be just in certain regions or everywhere. In that case it shall be up to the leaders of the Church to decide whether or not such deacons are to be constrained by the holy law of celibacy.[11]

Philips's careful language did nothing to dampen the controversy that surfaced during the council debate. It is particularly remarkable that so many participants chose to speak about the diaconate question in the midst of the divisive debate about collegiality.[12] The supporters of a permanent diaconate could now appeal to the aims that Pope John had set for the council in his opening address. If this council was to have an important pastoral aim, how could the participants refuse to allow some bishops the help they said was so desperately needed? Ordaining permanent deacons would also further the council's commitment to ecumenism by bringing Roman practice into line with that of the Orthodox and some of the Eastern Rite churches.[13]

In the council hall proponents of the diaconate sought to achieve consensus by toning down or omitting some of the more controversial arguments used by the activists and theologians. The speakers generally did not highlight the idea that ordaining deacons would give the clergy as a whole a much-needed orientation to service.[14] Instead, they pointed to the practical assis-

44

tance that deacons could offer overworked priests, who would be able to delegate some pastoral and administrative tasks.[15] Far from emphasizing the positive significance of marriage within the ordained clergy, the proponents conceded potential problems but offered reassurance: sacramental grace would strengthen married deacons to meet the challenge; the contrast between priests and deacons actually would place celibacy in higher esteem among the faithful.[16] Cardinal Julius Döpfner of Munich, in a speech drafted by Karl Rahner, minimized the aspect of innovation in the diaconate proposal by arguing that it did not even go as far as the Council of Trent. The earlier council, he argued, had treated the revival of the diaconate as a necessity, whereas the Philips document envisioned only a future possibility.[17] This argument employs a rather creative reading of Trent, as we saw earlier.

Another strategy aimed at consensus was to stress that acceptance amounted to no more than a possibility. The Church would impose permanent deacons on no one; bishops would have the option of ordaining them if local conditions should warrant it. And even if the Church allowed deacons to be married, celibacy might be retained in particular regions, or required of some candidates, particularly men under a certain age.[18]

Those who objected to the idea of married deacons were not reassured. They recognized that the proposal was limited in scope, but they saw this as an opportunity to remove it from the agenda. Insisting that the diaconate was merely a "disciplinary" matter—a question of church organization and regulation—Cardinal Francis Spellman of New York argued that it should not be incorporated into "On the Church," which was a "dogmatic" pronouncement—one that was addressing fundamental teachings.[19] If the opponents were able to move statements about a permanent diaconate into a decree with a more limited aim, the new institution would have a weaker foothold and they might limit or abort its ultimate implementation. In the best case they hoped to remove the matter from the council entirely and send it back to gather dust in the Holy Office.

The opponents of a permanent diaconate did recognize the practical need to extend the work of the clergy, and they had to respond to Pope John's call for a pastoral dimension in the council's work. But they wanted to do this in a way that would change the settled practice of the last millennium as little as possible, and that would be consistent with their vision of the Church. They therefore proposed other solutions to the pastoral problems—moves that they claimed would carry fewer risks, involve less disruption and controversy, and strengthen existing institutions. For example, the Church could ordain brothers in religious orders as deacons; these men, after all, were already performing many "diaconal" functions.[20] Or ordination might be offered to members of secular institutes—organizations that had been growing in popularity during the 1950s, in which men and women took the traditional monastic vows of poverty, chastity, and (usually) obedience, but continued to work and live in the secular world. Since the existing institutes aimed at the practice of spirituality and devotion, it would be necessary to create new institutes for the work of deacons, but these could be modeled on an already tested pattern.[21] Other suggestions involved instituting forms of lay "commissioning" that stopped short of ordination. For example, suggested Cardinal Ottaviani, the Church might reinvigorate the minor orders of acolyte and lector by conferring them on laymen who were doing committed apostolic work. Or those laymen could be given specific, recognized Church offices for defined periods of time.[22]

All of these solutions to contemporary pastoral problems presupposed that celibacy remained a necessary characteristic of the clergy. Some speakers, in fact, were willing to accept the idea of a permanent diaconate open to celibate men only. It is difficult to judge when this position was merely tactical and when it was being offered in earnest. Most council participants must have recognized that men who entered the diaconate and made a vow of celibacy would, in many cases, opt to move on to the priesthood, or would be encouraged to do so by their bishops. Thus, restricting the office of deacon to celibate men might result in no substantial change from the current practice—just the outcome the opponents hoped for. But some bishops, including several from Africa, seem to envision celibate deacons as holding a true office, requiring less formation than the priesthood but charged with important pastoral work—something like lay brothers in a religious order, but attached to a diocese.[23]

Virtually every opponent of reestablishing the diaconate pointed to the dangers of ordaining noncelibate men. Though aware of the theological arguments for celibacy, the bishops now stressed practical consequences. The Church would be tarnished with the scandals that would arise in some deacons' families—in fact this had already happened, according to one Yugoslav bishop, in the Eastern churches.[24] The number of men attracted to the priesthood would plummet, said Cardinal Antonio Bacci of the curia, because young men would choose the "easy way."[25] The faithful would be encouraged to question the importance of celibacy for priests, and this would weaken the whole clergy. The European press lent some weight to this last point by using the conciliar debates about the diaconate to air the whole question of priestly celibacy.[26]

The really striking development in the council hall, compared with the earlier debate among theologians and activists, is that speakers from outside Europe now played a key role. Many of the bishops from Latin America, Africa, and Asia spoke for entire episcopal conferences or at least for numerous colleagues. Latin American bishops such as Cardinal Juan Ladázuri-Ricketts of Lima, Peru, offered strong and coordinated support for married deacons.[27] Those from Africa and Asia generally wanted a permanent diaconate, but were divided about the requirement for celibacy.[28] The kinds of challenges these Church leaders faced—poverty, scattered communities, political persecution, a scarcity of priests that was often acute—gave their pleas a special authority. Many were able to point to a virtual army of lay missionaries and catechists whose pastoral effectiveness might be strengthened by ordination to the diaconate. Because deacons could be recruited and formed more quickly than priests, particularly in conditions of persecution, argued Bishop Paul Yü Pin of Nanjing, China, the missionary churches would be able to use the diaconate to build up a native clergy.[29] The forceful speeches by bishops from these regions must have swayed some participants who had not already made up their minds before the debate began. Bishop Jorge Kemerer of Posades, Argentina, speaking for twenty-five Latin American bishops, summed up their appeal in his peroration on October 14: "This is our great hope. The door is open—you need not enter it if you do not wish to, but do not close it on us!"[30]

COMPROMISE AND DECISION

In a procedural move that proved controversial but went ahead in the end, the full session was given the opportunity, on October 30, 1963, to vote on four propositions about collegiality and one on the diaconate, addressing the broad areas of disagreement about chapter 2 of the Philips document. The results would guide the next round of drafting. The proposition dealing with the diaconate called for a document "that considers the opportuneness of instituting the diaconate as a distinct and permanent grade of the sacred ministry, according to the needs of the Church in various regions."[31] This formulation recognized the elements of regional variation and opposition by allowing a less than universal implementation, while avoiding direct mention of the most controversial issue—celibacy. The proposition passed by a 75 percent margin, reflecting general support for the diaconate proposal already seen during the preparatory stages of the council.[32] The support had also been evident during the debate because, unlike most of the opponents, who spoke for themselves, many of the proponents represented significant groups or whole conferences of bishops. The number of colleagues represented by individual speakers would be noted by the subcommittee in charge of drafting the next round of "On the Church," and this would lend greater weight to the arguments of the proponents in the next draft.[33]

During the late fall of 1963 and through the spring of 1964, the various subcommittees completed their work and a text of "On the Church," under the overall drafting supervision of Msgr. Philips, was accepted by the Doctrinal Commission. Before the chapter on bishops, priests, and deacons was presented to the full council at its third session in the fall of 1964 for a final vote (no further debate was allowed), Msgr. Philips boiled down the basic points at issue into thirty-nine propositions that would be voted on. The last five concerned the diaconate, and the final three addressed the matters that had been broadly controversial.

Question 37 made the procedures for implementation more specific by assigning them to individual episcopal conferences with the approval of the pope. The idea of giving such an important role to bishops' conferences turned out to be fairly controversial: 702 votes (32 percent) registered against, and it is easy to see why. The proposal really amounted to collegiality in practice, and the regional variations that would result from it would reverse the policy of Roman centralism that some participants at the council believed to be critical for the unity of the Church. Moreover, the entire machinery of episcopal conferences, which are such a feature of Catholic life today, barely existed in many parts of the world in 1964.[34] In general, the conferences had developed most strongly in the newer or expanding churches, including that of the United States, but had very limited functions or vitality in places where diocesan organization had been firmly implanted for centuries.[35] The compromise allowing regional implementation "according to need," then, addressed, in theory at least, the regional diversity of both views and pastoral situations expressed in the debate. But to strict opponents of the permanent diaconate the result was unsatisfactory from the standpoint of both process and result.

The final two questions introduced the really hot topic: celibacy. Question 38 provided that the pope might allow the ordination of married men "of a mature age" to the diaconate. This proposition passed with slightly less opposition than the previous question, gaining a 72 percent majority. Question 39 tested the limit case: whether the pope might allow young men to become deacons without a vow of celibacy. The Doctrinal Commission's document had taken a negative position on this, and the council voted no by a 62 percent majority.[36]

These last two questions encapsulate the compromise on celibacy that the Doctrinal Commission had reached during the winter of 1963–64. The requirement of celibacy for younger men aimed to ensure that the diaconate should not become the "easy road" into the ordained clergy, draining potential recruits away from the priesthood. At the same time, the African and Asian bishops who had asked for a celibate diaconate as a way to build up a native clergy would have a chance to try out their proposal; no region would be required to permit even "mature" deacons to marry. Allowing the ordination of men who were already married, although an important departure from almost a thousand years of Western practice, brought Catholic practice into conformity with the early Church and with the longstanding tradition of most other Christian denominations. The exact definitions of "young" and "mature age" were left open, allowing the pope to determine them later. Paul VI decided on thirty-five as the minimum "mature age" when providing norms for the diaconate in 1967.[37]

Once the votes on individual propositions were completed, the council moved to adopt the entire third chapter of the document "On the Church" in two parts, the second containing the diaconate proposal. Seventy-six percent voted for the draft as it stood.[38] This document, with only a few minor changes in wording, became Section 29 of *Lumen Gentium*, adopted by the council on November 21, 1964.

LUMEN GENTIUM 29: REFORM, CONTINUITY, AND CAUTION

The handling of the diaconate in this section bears the marks of the council's debates and compromises, which themselves reflected the broader struggle between the goals of reform/renewal and continuity/tradition.[39] Section 29, part of chapter 3 in the final version rather than chapter 2, comes at the end of the chapter's top-down treatment of the clergy, after a long discussion about bishops and a shorter presentation of the priesthood. Here is the section in full:

At a lower level of the hierarchy stand the deacons, on whom hands are laid "not for the priesthood, but for the ministry." For, strengthened by sacramental grace, they serve the people of God in the ministry of the liturgy, of the word and of charity, in communion with the bishop and his priests. To the extent that competent authorities shall give him these assignments, the deacon is to administer baptism solemnly, to reserve and distribute the eucharist, to assist at and bless marriages in the name of the church, to bring the eucharist to the dying, to read Holy Scripture to the faithful, to teach and exhort the people, to preside at the worship and prayer of the faithful, to act as minister for blessings and devotions, and to preside at funeral services and burials. Dedicated to the works of charity and administration, deacons should remember the admonition given by the blessed Polycarp: "...compassionate, careful, and walking according to the truth of the Lord, who became the servant of all."

These tasks are exceedingly necessary for the life of the church. Yet in many regions they can be carried out only with difficulty, given the present structure of the Latin church. Therefore, the diaconate may be restored in the future as a distinct and permanent grade of the hierarchy. It will fall, however, to the various kinds of episcopal conferences that are responsible for particular regions to decide, with the approval of the pope, whether and where it is opportune to appoint such deacons for pastoral needs. With the consent of the pope this diaconate may be conferred on men of a mature age, even if they are married, and also on suitable younger men; but for these the law of celibacy must remain in force.[40]

The elements of reform supported by majority votes in the council are clearly expressed here: the diaconate can become a permanent ministry, and celibacy need not be required for men of mature age. The compromises are apparent, too: this ministry will only be adopted in regions where episcopal conferences request it and the pope approves; and celibacy will continue to be required for younger men. The text also gives a range of tasks for deacons that obviously go well beyond those listed in the 1917 Code of Canon Law.[41] Various writers and council speakers had argued that having deacons perform one or another of these functions would respond to pastoral needs, and the text reflects their suggestions. The preponderance of liturgical and catechetical functions in the list particularly reflects the expressed needs of Latin American bishops, who hoped to give deacons broad pastoral roles in areas rarely visited by priests.[42] The list, however, is merely illustrative, and the assignment of particular tasks is up to "competent authorities," leaving open the possibility that they might be limited in practice. And, of course, the reliance on episcopal conferences with papal approval for implementation leaves open the possibility that, in the end, the revival of the diaconate might be carried out only in a very limited way.

The text shows notable caution, too, about any change in the traditional view of the clergy as involving an ascent through grades. The diaconate as a step to priesthood remains untouched, continuing alongside this permanent ministry. More broadly, the grades of the clergy are strongly confirmed: chapter 3 moves from bishop to priest to deacon in the framework of increasing limitations, and the very first reference to the deacon here is to his "lower level." The key phrase "not for priesthood, but for ministry" is chosen, in part, to underline just this point. The formula comes from the ancient ordination rites, where in its earliest form the deacon is ordained "for the ministry of [or service to] the bishop, to do what is ordered by him."[43] Significantly, the text here chooses to quote later ordination rituals, in which the direct relation to the bishop, characteristic of ancient deacons, has dropped out, precisely to avoid the impression that both deacons and priests may serve the bishop directly and in an analogous way. Indeed, the handling of this quote implies that the ministry of the new deacons will be performed, like that of transitional deacons, under the supervision of priests rather than the bishop. This is just what has happened in most cases. Even the participation of the diaconate in the Sacrament of Holy Orders is implied rather than affirmed in the phrase "strengthened by sacramental grace."[44]

Lumen Gentium 29 is also circumspect about providing any theological rationale for the diaconate as a permanent ministry, a reticence that is hardly surprising after the heated debate. There is no mention of a need for ordained ministers whose lives would be shared more closely with the laity, or for ministers who could bridge an assumed gap between the higher clergy and the rest of the people of God.[45] One finds no suggestion that the Church should use its sacramental grace to strengthen its ministry, a view that, if taken to its logical conclusion, would argue that the diaconate should be revived in the universal Church, opposition notwithstanding.[46] As a rationale, the text cites the difficulty of carrying out pastoral tasks "given the present structure of the Latin Church," an allusion to the shortage of priests in some areas, with a nod to ancient and Eastern Rite practices as a possible model for correcting it. The brevity and reticence of this chapter leave a wide area open to future debate and exploration about who deacons should be within the ministry and in the Church, and how their tasks might work out in practice.

Despite its brevity, however, *Lumen Gentium* 29 does provide a sketch of diaconal identity, one that points to the image of Christ the servant. This understanding emerges from a careful reading of the text itself within the structure, style, and major themes in this Constitution and related council documents—the subject of the next chapter.

CHAPTER 5

• • • • • •

VATICAN II

Servant Ministers for a Servant Church

We have seen that in the debate about the diaconate before the council, proponents and opponents of the proposal framed their arguments from within different visions of the Church and of ministry. One vision of the Church and its ministers, in which they are seen through the lens of servanthood, had already helped to frame the view of deacons as service ministers among proponents of a revived diaconate before the council. The view of the Church itself as servant also appealed to many of the council participants and their theological advisors. While by no means the only key to understanding the Church found in the council documents, the servant metaphor gained prominence in some of the most important texts and proved to be decisive in sketching a ministerial identity for the deacon.

THE CHURCH AS SERVANT

This twentieth-century way of understanding the Church involved a significant development from earlier views. The New Testament and early Christian writers understood the Church to be the vehicle for Christ's continuing service to the world through the Holy Spirit, but they did not see the Church itself as exemplifying Christ the servant.[1] They preferred metaphors like the Body of Christ, the household of God, the assembly of the saints, and similar images that stressed the solidarity of a mission group that was already weak and "servile" enough in its social context—small, vulnerable, and struggling to survive and grow.[2] In such conditions, a community call to servanthood would hardly suggest itself.

The contemporary Roman Catholic diaconate, as it developed before and during Vatican II, arose in a very different situation. In the mid-twentieth century, the Catholic Church was a worldwide institution with considerable power in the public realm, and it still functioned as the legally established church in many countries. The clergy were largely defined by their exercise of governance and of the "sacred power" to administer the sacraments. The reform impulse that animated the council sought to shift the focus away from what Bishop Emiel-Jozef de Smedt of Bruges, Belgium, in an intervention early in the first session, called "clericalism, juridicism, and triumphalism"[3]—attributes against which the early Church hardly needed to be warned. This reforming movement at the council was tempered in the debates and documents by a commitment to continuity in the Church's doctrine and practice. We have seen how that dynamic contributed to the final content of *Lumen Gentium* 29.

The animating idea behind the vision of a servant Church is that, if the Church is to represent Christ and carry on Christ's ongoing mission in the world, then the Church itself must exemplify and act in accordance with Christ's character as servant. *Lumen Gentium*, in its opening section on "The Mystery of the Church," passes through a range of Old Testament metaphors pointing to the Church; coming to Christ, the constitution frames the mystery in terms of humble servanthood:

> Just as Jesus Christ accomplished the work of redemption in poverty and persecution, so is the Church called to go forward on the same path, that she may share with humanity the fruits of salvation. Christ Jesus, "though he was in the form of God...emptied himself, taking the form of a slave" (Philippians 2:6–7); and for our sake, "though he was rich, he made himself poor" (2 Corinthians 8:9). Likewise, the Church, though it

needs human resources to perform its mission, is not raised up to seek after earthly glory, but to express humility and self-denial through her own example as well.[4]

Going further, the Pastoral Constitution on the Church in the Modern World *Gaudium et Spes* (December 7, 1965) concludes its prefatory statement:

The Church...intends only one thing: through the guidance of the Paraclete, to carry on the work of Christ Himself, who came into the world to give witness to the truth, to save and not to judge, to serve and not to be served.[5]

The outward-turning thrust of this constitution, and its engagement with the contemporary world in all its variegated manifestations, draws out a particularly clear vision of the servant Church. Thus, in a development beyond strictly scriptural, medieval, or early modern views, the Church is seen as not only serving Christ and the Spirit, but also the broader world; and not just by witnessing to the truth and acting as a vehicle of grace, but by seeking peace, justice, the common good, and the brotherhood of all peoples. Moreover, the Church is to carry out this mission in a self-giving way, as a humble servant; not triumphalist or authoritarian, but in respectful dialogue with the world, always ready to offer help and solace. Paul VI captured the idea succinctly in his closing homily for the council in 1965: "The rich abundance of [the council's] teaching looks in one direction, that it might serve the human person....The church has, so to speak, declared herself the servant of humankind."[6]

The council's appeal to an idea of the Church itself as exemplifying Christ the servant parallels a theme that pervades the council's treatment of the Church's internal ordering, and especially its treatment of the clergy. This is a shift in emphasis, compared with preconciliar treatments of the clergy, from power to service. Thus, *Lumen Gentium* begins its chapter 3, on the clergy, by stating, "Ministers invested with sacred power are at the service of their brothers and sisters."[7] The shift does not mean that the Catholic clergy have ceased to be defined to an important extent by their powers and faculties in the sacramental realm or in pastoral oversight. The council, however, clearly ties those powers to the ideal of service: the clergy are first and foremost servants of the whole Church, the people of God. Only servant ministers could direct and exemplify a servant Church.

Despite framing the clergy as servants in a broad and important sense, the council did not, and really could not, present the whole clergy as exemplifying Christ the servant. The council's emphases on leadership as humble service and on the clergy's mission to serve the people of God do reflect the image of Christ the servant, just as they parallel the ideal of a servant Church. But the service the clergy is called to provide, specifically the three tasks assigned to them—to teach, sanctify, and govern—take us into different metaphorical spaces.[8] These tasks distill into the specific realm of ministry three other images of Christ imprinted on every Christian disciple at baptism: prophet, priest, and king.

What happened to the image of Christ the servant in the treatment of the clergy at Vatican II? The image remained integral to the clergy by coming to rest on the revived office of deacon. Although this theme was not prominent in the council debates, the connection between Christ the servant, deacons as servant ministers, and the Church as servant was powerfully expressed by Bishop José Clemente Maurer, CSsR, of Sucre, Bolivia, representing forty other bishops in a speech on October 10, 1963:

> The diaconate should be restored so that the Church may acquire and express a clearer understanding of its nature, appearing to all as the handmaid of Christ, ever with great love remaining in, and giving its testimony for, God's Servant in His humility....The diaconate, according to the common doctrine in its fullness, imprints a permanent and indelible character. They truly are better priests and bishops who live according to the grace and character of the diaconate, seeking nothing other than to serve at the lowest grade. For this reason, it is desirable that legislation in the Western Church

should be renewed in a way that makes the ambition to ascend to the priesthood in no way a condition for ordination to the diaconate. Such [a renewed] legislation and practice, which protects and elevates the diaconate in its humility, will be a continual admonition to the higher grades [of the clergy], that they ought to exceed the deacons themselves in the practice of humility. Indeed, as it is the duty of the council to check errors which darken the form of the Church in the eyes of others, and to do so in a positive way, this [renewal] stands up most effectively against that most deadly error into which they fall who treat the priesthood as though it were an honor acquired for self-glorification, a step in an ecclesiastical career.[9]

This speech expresses some ideas that contribute to *Lumen Gentium* 29, as well as some of the more ambitious hopes for the future diaconate as a force for renewal in the Church. The final text, as we saw in the last chapter, is more reticent, cautious, and indeed also more positive in tone; there is no criticism of clerical careerism or anything else.[10] But the image of Christ the servant does come through clearly in the text itself.

THE COUNCIL TEXTS: INTRODUCING CHRIST THE SERVANT

The task of sketching an overall framework for the diaconate, consistent with the structure, rhetoric, and outlook of *Lumen Gentium* as a whole, fell to the drafter, Gérard Philips, whom we have encountered already in connection with the votes and drafts of 1962–64. As a key to interpreting the carefully worded two-paragraph text of *Lumen Gentium* 29, already quoted in the last chapter, we have the report (called a *Relatio*) from the drafting committee presenting this section to the full council in 1964. We can also consult Philips's own commentary on *Lumen Gentium*, published in 1967. Using these interpretive keys along with a close reading of the text itself, a distinctive image emerges of the deacon as representing Christ the servant. This becomes clear if we recognize what the text emphasizes in the key sentences of the first paragraph: specifically, the opening, the closing, and the language that makes deacons distinctive within chapter 3's presentation of the clergy as a whole.

This chapter assigns three tasks to the clergy: to teach, sanctify, and govern the people of God.[11] The way in which section 29 handles the third task shows how diaconal identity is envisioned. As we move through the chapter from bishops to priests, the three tasks are exercised with increasing limitations. For deacons, the scope of the first two tasks is further limited, as sanctifying and teaching become "the ministry of the liturgy, [and] of the Word." But for the third task we find a complete substitution: governing is replaced by "charity."[12] Read within chapter 3 as a whole, the point is clear. Deacons do not govern; instead, they perform works of charity. The substitution serves to stress the importance of this task for deacons and the fact that its exercise is in some way distinctive of diaconal office.

A few lines later, the text returns to the three tasks, and this time, picking up the thread that the third task has to do with governance, the document qualifies and expands its earlier statement by admitting a form of diaconal leadership next to the works of charity. Before this, the text has listed nine functions that deacons may perform, all of which are within the ministries of the word and of liturgy. But in summing up, the text returns to the third task, describing the deacon as "dedicated to the works of charity and administration."[13] The conclusion: deacons clearly have all three tasks to perform, yet what is distinctive about them compared with bishops and priests is a focus, already stressed, on works of charity, placed together now with a qualitatively different, subordinate form of leadership in the Church—not governing (*regere*), the word used for bishops and priests, but administration (*administratio*). This word denotes an organizational role more concerned with implementation than with policy, and where any exercise of leadership over others is limited and performed under supervision.[14] In the tasks of teaching and sanctifying, then, deacons are simply more limited than bishops and priests. But in the focus on works of charity and on the limited and supervised exercise of leadership, deacons are distinctive—indeed unique—within the clergy. The drafting committee's report to the council supports this reading, noting that the list of liturgical and catechetical tasks, though given relatively long treatment, is intended to be illustrative but not definitive for diaconal ministry. The distinctive aspect of the diaconate, the report affirms, is the dedication to charity and administration.[15]

The opening and closing of the key paragraph in *Lumen Gentium* 29 further stress the deacon's identity as servant. The paragraph opens by highlighting the diaconate's "lower level" within the clergy and its character as ministry or service (*ministerium*) rather than priesthood. This opening sentence already emphasizes the humble status and limited power in the sacramental and pastoral spheres that are to characterize deacons.[16] Their place in the clergy is to be servants of others, particularly the bishop; and to minister to others' needs. This vision is distilled and given greater weight in the paragraph's conclusion, which uses the quote from Polycarp we examined in chapter 2, exhorting deacons to walk in the truth of the Lord, who became the servant [*minister*] of all." The footnote explains that Polycarp's own word here is *diakonos*, thus equating "deacon" with "servant."[17]

The Decree on Missionary Activity, *Ad Gentes*, adopted in the following year, 1965, takes up this teaching but places the deacon in a new context:

> Where it seems opportune to episcopal conferences, the order of the diaconate as a permanent state of life should be restored, according to the Constitution on the Church. There are men who are already exercising what is really a deacon's ministry—preaching the Word of God as teachers, leading far-flung Christian communities in the name of the bishop or parish priest, or practicing charity in social or charitable works. It would indeed give help to these men if they were strengthened and bound more closely to the altar by the laying on of hands which has come down to us from the apostles, so that, through the sacramen-

tal grace of the diaconate, they may be able to perform their ministry more effectively.[18]

While *Ad Gentes* adds to the council's presentation of deacons by addressing the missionary situation, *Lumen Gentium*'s framework of the deacon as servant is carried into this later document. The missionary decree does present deacons as "leading [*moderantes*] far-flung Christian communities," which suggests a somewhat broader scope for leadership than is implied in the "administration" of *Lumen Gentium* 29. But deacons do this only "in the name of a parish priest or bishop," so the limitations and the stress on supervision are retained. *Ad Gentes* also places somewhat more emphasis on the catechetical role of deacons, but as in *LG* 29, works of charity substitute for governing as their third task, highlighting the distinctive diaconal calling to charitable works.

Why did the council document frame the diaconate by highlighting works of charity, limitations on power, and a servant identity? The latter two emphases clearly had some practical underpinnings: the council had no intention of defining diaconal office in a way that could set up any possible rivalry with priests or bishops.[19] But beyond that, these themes present the deacon as a clear representative, within the clergy, of the evolving idea of a servant Church, itself understood as the representative of Christ the servant.

In the years since the council, among theologians, Church authorities, and formation directors, this sketch of the deacon as representing Christ the servant has been further developed, becoming the dominant understanding of diaconal identity. But the broader debate about the diaconate that began before the council has continued up to the present, pointing in other directions as well, as we will see in the next chapter.

CHAPTER SIX

• • • • • •

THE SEARCH FOR DIACONAL IDENTITY SINCE THE COUNCIL

Vatican II gave the worldwide Church a brief, cautious charter for the diaconate, together with a skeleton sketch for an identity of this office modeled on Christ the servant. In the years that followed, the Church took all this in slowly, incompletely, and with wide variations by region. The reception of the council's vision in this case parallels the Church's struggle to implement, and even to understand, the council's vision and teaching.[1] For the diaconate, that implementation was particularly uneven because *Lumen Gentium* 29 left it to regional bishops' conferences to decide what to do. This chapter reviews how Church leaders, deacons, and theologians have fleshed out their understandings of who deacons are and what they are tasked to do since the council. We conclude with an assessment of where that conversation stands today.

A HALTING AND INCOMPLETE ACCEPTANCE

In the years immediately following the council, most conferences did nothing. The practical obstacles brought up before and during the council by opponents of the renewed diaconate had not gone away, after all. The problem of teaching and forming candidates outside the seminary system, usually in contexts with no tradition of nonclerical theological education, proved—and indeed has continued to prove—particularly daunting. This problem was exacerbated by the lack of a clear job description for which candidates should be trained and formed. There was no model in the Latin Church for members of the clergy who were committed to a permanent and indeed sacramentally grounded ministry but might typically earn their livelihoods elsewhere. How would that work in practice? Once ordained and assigned, how could such ministers be supported and supervised? The most obvious departure from long practice, of course, was the inclusion of married men in the clergy. How would the faithful react to this, what effect would it have on the requirement of celibacy for priests and bishops—might it reduce vocations to the priesthood?

Theological objections to the diaconate, based as they were on long-held views of the Church and of ministry, did not go away either. The council taught that bishops were ordained to the "fullness of order," thus shifting away from the identification of holy orders specifically with priesthood and the power to celebrate the Eucharist.[2] Yet that traditional priestly view of orders was too well-grounded among bishops, priests, and seminary professors to change overnight. And if this is the meaning of the sacrament of orders, why ordain "service ministers"?

Even the idea that the diaconate is a sacrament, assumed and certainly strongly implied in *Lumen Gentium* and *Ad Gentes*, was not explicitly defined in these texts and was considered an open question among a few theologians until a stream of official documents, together with the fact of tens of thousands of diaconal ordinations, effectively decided the matter.[3] Nevertheless, the lack of a set of defined functions unique to deacons and not shared by priests or all the faithful clouded the picture of diaconal identity. All of the tasks in word and sacrament performed by deacons are also the province of priests, and many of a deacon's functions can also be done by any of the lay faithful. Through this lens, the diaconate looks superfluous. Accordingly, some theologians wondered if Vatican II avoided the challenge of building a stronger priesthood and lay apostolate by opting for what George Tavard called "a minor restructuring of ministry," the revived diaconate, instead.[4] As we will see in the next chapter, this criticism relies on a narrowly functional understanding of the diaconate, and also posits a false "either-or" in envisioning a renewal of ministry by priests, deacons, and the nonordained faithful, as though they could not be renewed together, indeed in communion with each other. But this critique does capture and express the confusion about what exactly deacons were (and are) tasked to do, a confusion that contributed to the hesitation about pushing ahead with this new ministry in many parts of the world.

STEPPING INTO THE BREACH: THE DEACON AS A MINIPRIEST

The regional churches in Western Europe and North America that did adopt the diaconate with gusto had in common a particular pastoral problem for which the diaconate could be seen as a partial, if only a partial, solution. All experienced a precipitous and continuing decline in the number of priests in the generation after the diaconate received its charter at Vatican II.[5] Fewer priests meant a void in pastoral ministries that the faithful had come to expect. In this context, deacons have been pressured to stand in as needed, especially with baptisms, funeral rites, weddings, visits to the homebound, and general pastoral care. As a result of these immediate pastoral needs, many priests and bishops, together with people in the pews who see deacons more often than not wearing vestments or clerical collars, have come to picture the deacon as a kind of minipriest.

Viewed from the framework of Vatican II, then, the diaconate in its first generation developed in an unexpected direction. In the first place, the office that was envisioned to symbolize the servant Church, especially in its focus on the needy and the marginalized, grew almost entirely in the world's richest countries, in part because those societies could provide the resources, both financial and educational, to support the new ministry.

(Even in the richest countries, of course, many people are poor and marginalized; a ministry whose center of gravity is in works of charity is still very much needed.) Second, when *Lumen Gentium* 29 alluded to the shortage of priests as a primary rationale for ordaining deacons, the document was referring to places in the world where the shortage was then acute. This was mainly in mission lands, in rural areas, or in places where the Church was lightly planted. But in the first generation after the council, it was a *drop* in the number of priests within well-established church institutions that created a pastoral crisis, a new void, into which deacons were called to step. The result, in the way deacons have been seen and to an extent have understood themselves, often has been the blurry picture of a priest's helper, rather than a ministerial identity grounded in the unique and integral combination of liturgy, word, and charity envisioned by Vatican II.[6]

THE DIACONATE AS BRIDGE OR "INTERMEDIATE ORDER": PICKING UP THE THREAD

In chapter 3 we encountered a view of the diaconate that developed in the years before the council, pointing toward a role for the office that had the potential to counterbalance this pull toward minipriesthood. That line of thought envisioned the deacon as a bridge between the higher clergy and the faithful as a whole, a minister permanently and sacramentally in service to the Church through ordination, but normally residing and earning a livelihood outside the rectory, religious order, or other church institution. Whatever the details of putting such a vision into practice, this approach points outside the model of minipriesthood and gives one dimension of the fuller image of the deacon as minister of the threshold that will be developed in chapter 9.

The vision of the deacon as a bridge figure, though put forward in a number of council speeches, never appeared in the final documents, either as a framework for diaconal identity or as a rationale for reviving the office as a permanent ministry.

However, Paul VI, setting out guidelines for the diaconate in *Ad Pascendum* (1972), took up the theme, writing that Vatican II had restored the diaconate

> as an intermediate order between the higher levels of the ecclesiastical hierarchy and the rest of the People of God, being as it were an interpreter of the needs and desires of the Christian communities, [and with the aim of] stimulating the Church's service or, [as one may say,] *diakonia*, in the local Christian communities.[7]

This brief formulation suggests that a deacon, by living among the "rest of the People of God," will be in a good position to inform priests and bishops of the people's needs.[8] And, because he lives so closely among them, the deacon, representing the clergy, is in a position to animate the people to deeper involvement in the Church's mission. It is worth noting that the deacon's role is pictured within the Church, and not as an apostolate to the wider world. Although brief, this treatment of the diaconate as a kind of bridge is clear enough to suggest how it might become a dimension of diaconal identity. The specific term *intermediate order* is subject to misunderstanding, however, since it could be taken to suggest that deacons have not received the same sacrament of holy orders as priests and bishops. As a result, this term has not entered into the general theological conversation touching on the diaconate as a bridge or threshold ministry.[9]

Theologians after the council continued to explore the bridge theme in fruitful ways. Yves Congar, in a 1965 essay, uses a starting point in liturgy. He notes that, in the Eastern Rites where deacons have a significant role, the deacon acts as a mediator between the celebrant and the people, especially where the liturgical action takes place at a distance from the worshipers, usually behind a screen. Developing from this, Congar envisions diaconal ministry as one of mediation between the Church and everyday life, between "the sacred structures of the Church and the activities that involve contact with the world." More concretely, he imagines deacons with a special mission to those "who are drawn to the church but cannot quite get there" and who constitute "a kind of catechumenal church, a church of the threshold and of the borderland."[10] Also in 1965, Henri Denis, proposing a distinction between priesthood and diaconate, gave a dynamic, outward-moving quality to diaconal ministry that is highly suggestive: "Whereas the priesthood, because of its presiding role with respect to Word and Eucharist, is the sign of a church always 'given' by Christ within the world, the diaconate is rather the sign, in the world, of a church in the making through God's grace."[11]

In this view the distinctive role of the priest is to gather the eucharistic assembly, whereas deacons, from an integral but assisting location within that gathering, are especially tasked to be a vehicle of its graces beyond the everyday faithful to the wider world, the sign of a "church in the making." Both Congar and Denis, then, give the diaconate a particular mission focus as a bridge beyond the Church as presently constituted.[12] Particularly in French-speaking countries and in Latin America, an understanding of the diaconate specifically as a ministry aimed at the margins of the Church or the marginalized of society continued to develop in the following decades.[13] One expression for this vision of the diaconate has been a ministry of the threshold, a term we have borrowed and expanded upon in developing the second model proposed in this book.

In 2003, the Vatican's International Theological Commission noted a range of theological ideas that present the deacon in a bridge or mediating role "between clergy and laity, between the church and the world, between the liturgy and ordinary life, between charitable activities and the Eucharist, [or] between the center and the periphery of the Christian community."[14] By gathering these "in-between" aspects of diaconal ministry within the unifying concept of bridging or mediation, the Commission acknowledged their theological richness and interconnections, but did not develop any theological or pastoral implications from them.[15] Nor did the Commission connect them to the evolving understanding of the diaconate as a ministry distinctly aimed at the margins of Church and society. Chapter 9 integrates all these various insights about diaconal identity into a single, rounded model: ministry of the threshold. During the first generation after the council, however, this overall approach to the diaconate remained in the background, owing to the lack of a starting point in any council document, as well as a need to ground the bridge/mediation/threshold idea in real ministerial experience, which was still at an early stage.

CHRIST THE SERVANT

At the same time, the identification of the diaconate with service or servanthood, however vaguely defined, became the default position in official documents, theological studies, and popular presentations of the deacon's ministry. This framework develops out of the sketch of diaconal identity modeled on Christ the servant in *Lumen Gentium* 29, and it retains from that text the stress on works of charity as most characteristic of the deacon. Chapter 8 will analyze this vision of diaconal identity in detail, attempting to give it a level of both theological rigor and practical usefulness that is lacking in overly general appeals to this theme, which continue to be common today. But even when loosely defined, a diaconal identity modeled on Christ the servant offered something distinctive compared with priesthood, and so provided a counterweight to the pull toward minipriesthood that resulted from the pastoral crisis in the regions where the diaconate first took root.

A brief survey of official documents and papal addresses illustrates the central importance of this theme in the way Church leaders defined the ministerial identity of deacons in the first generation after the council. In 1972, Paul VI, in the same document, *Ad Pascendum*—actually, in the same sentence— where he described the diaconate as an "intermediate order," also affirms it to be "a sign or sacrament of the Lord Christ himself, who came not to be served, but to serve." Pope St. John Paul II, in a 1985 address to the Italian Diaconate Convention, roots the diaconate more clearly in the sacrament of holy orders, affirming that "the deacon, participating in the triple function of the sacrament of Orders, personifies in his degree Christ as Servant of the Father."[16]

The Catechism of the Catholic Church (1997) develops this model further in the same direction: "The Sacrament of Holy Orders marks [deacons] with an imprint ('character') which cannot be removed and which configures them to Christ, who made himself the 'deacon' or servant of all."[17] The text quotes here the same sentence from Polycarp that *Lumen Gentium* 29 used as the culminating image of its first paragraph. But the *Catechism* conceptualizes Polycarp's metaphor in the more specific terms of sacramental theology, presenting the model of Christ the servant as a sacramental character, something permanent that is conferred by the sacrament of orders, just as baptism and confirmation are understood to confer a more general Christian character. Within the *Catechism*, this way of framing the diaconate may flow in part from its placement within the section on sacraments, but we see a broader tendency in Church documents to harmonize the model of Christ the servant with a traditional theology of holy orders in which the priest acts in the person of Christ when celebrating the Eucharist.

The *Basic Norms for the Formation of Permanent Deacons*, issued in 1998 by the Vatican's Congregation for Catholic Education, adopts a more general approach, noting that *Lumen Gentium* 29 and its quotation from Polycarp had "outline[d] the specific theological identity of the deacon: as a participant in the one ecclesiastical ministry, he is a specific sacramental sign, in the Church, of Christ the servant," and therefore, in his "specific spirituality...a living icon of Christ the servant within the Church."[18]

The ordination rite for deacons also stresses the theme of Christ the servant, and this framework was strengthened in the successive revisions undertaken after the council, in 1968 and 1990. In the current rite, immediately after invoking the Holy Spirit, the bishop prays that those being ordained may show "unfeigned love, concern for the sick and poor, unassuming authority," continuing several lines later, "so that by imitating on earth your Son, who came not to be served but to serve, he may be found worthy to reign in heaven with him."[19] The prayer includes two models for deacons: the Levites, ministers of the altar in the Old Testament, and the "seven men of good repute" from Acts 6:1–6, noting that "your Son's Apostles...by prayer and the laying on of hands...entrusted to these chosen men the ministry of serving at table."[20] This second model was added in the 1968 revision, clearly chosen to counterbalance the sole focus on liturgy in the earlier rite by highlighting the task of charity.[21] The 1990 revision continues this trend: small word changes replaced references to the office of deacon as an honor, choosing rather an emphasis on service.[22]

Theologians writing on the diaconate in the first generation and beyond have also laid a great stress on the deacon as servant, often appealing to the model of Christ the servant from Polycarp and *Lumen Gentium* 29. In part they are taking their cues from official documents, but there seem to be two other broad motivations behind this theological direction. The first comes from the German association of the diaconate with *Diakonie*, the translation of *diakonia* as loving service. The German supporters of the diaconate as a permanent ministry before Vatican II had understood charitable service as the central task of deacons, a task that would be restored to its place in the apostolic ministry, in the clergy itself, through deacons.[23] Through the first generation, this view, which of course found support in Church documents, was widely diffused, and influential in America as well.[24] The second reason the model of the deacon as servant won wide appeal was that it could be used to give a ministerial identity to the diaconate that was separate and distinct from priesthood, and of course this would undercut the tendency to picture deacons as minipriests.[25] This distinction has often been grounded in the opening line of *Lumen Gentium* 29, where the diaconate is "not for the priesthood, but for the ministry": an understanding of ministry is then developed around the idea of service.[26] Both of these theological underpinnings of the model of Christ the servant for deacons are valid points of departure. Chapter 8 below will engage the theological conversation about this model in detail.

What is missing from most treatments of the servant theme after the council is the framework for the diaconate that emerged from a reading of *Lumen Gentium* 29 in the context of that entire constitution along with *Gaudium et Spes*:

the deacon as the representative, within the clergy, of a servant Church, itself understood as a representative of Christ the servant.[27] Such an understanding of both Church and diaconate is to some extent assumed in the widespread emphasis on humble service and charity as the distinctive focus of diaconal ministry, but particularly in recent years this theme has not been clearly related to the image of Christ the servant, or explicitly rooted in any particular vision of the Church.[28] Instead, especially in the official documents, we find an attempt to harmonize the deacon's representation of Christ the servant with traditional ideas about the sacramental character conferred by holy orders, and indeed to see the office as personifying Christ the servant in a manner analogous to a priest's personifying Christ in the celebration of the Eucharist. Whether this analogy is coherent or useful for the diaconate is a question we will consider in the next chapter. Meanwhile, by the end of the first generation, the idea that deacons represent Christ the servant at all was running into some strong critical headwinds.

THE CRITICS

John N. Collins offered the first influential negative assessment in 1990, arguing that the focus on humble and charitable service in the dominant understanding of the diaconate had arisen from a simple misunderstanding of words. In an exhaustive study, Collins argued that the *diakon-* words used in early Christian literature, including *diakonia* and the word for a deacon, *diakonos,* do not have this sense at all, but refer to being sent out or acting on behalf of someone else. While not providing a specific critique of the model of Christ the servant, Collins's work undercuts the linguistic and, thereby, in his view, even the scriptural foundation for the view of diaconal ministry as humble service.[29]

More criticisms poured in from a theological direction. In 2003 the International Vatican's Theological Commission, while admitting that the theme of Christ the servant was well grounded in Church documents, found it "problematic" as a distinctive vision of the diaconate, mainly because "service must be considered as a characteristic common to every ordained ministry."[30] A range of other criticisms will be reviewed in chapter 8. Moreover, there has been a reluctance in some quarters to affirm for deacons any manner of representing Christ, on the grounds that this could prejudice the debate about ordaining women to the diaconate, since it has been argued that as women they could not represent Christ.[31]

MOVING BEYOND THE IMPASSE

By the early 2000s, conversation about the diaconate had reached an impasse about Christ the servant as a key to diaconal identity. On one side, there was a weight of Church documents, along with pastoral treatments and homilies, that treated this image as the most important key to the diaconate. Even today, a search of diocesan websites with any content about deacons shows that servanthood, and often Christ the servant explicitly, provide the usual framework for understanding who the deacon is.[32] In addition, many theological studies of the diaconate incorporate such a view within their broader arguments, and there is no lack of well-argued and pastorally informed treatments of diaconal ministry in which representation of Christ the servant provides the key.[33] But the supporters of this approach generally ignore the objections of the critics. Chapter 8 below addresses this impasse in the conversation by proposing a carefully defined treatment of Christ the servant as a fundamental key to diaconal identity and responds specifically to the critiques.

As some writers have moved away from seeing the diaconate through the image of Christ the servant, they have explored other themes, such as the deacon's social location in the "borderland" between Church and world, or his capacity to identify with, and so to represent, the outcast and the "other," and his role as a social intermediary. These explorations actually pick up and develop the insights of those who have seen the deacon as a bridge figure. Chapter 9 will gather these threads from the past sixty-five years into a single compelling image of the deacon as minister of the threshold.

In order to flesh out these two key images of a deacon's identity, however, it is important to begin from a solid foundation, specifically from a coherent account of diaconal ministry in all its dimensions. That is the subject of the next chapter.

CHAPTER SEVEN

• • • • • •

THE DIACONATE IN FULL

Three Dimensions

What makes a deacon? We often hear of deacons defined by what they can and cannot do, usually in comparison with a priest. Or, on the contrary, it is affirmed that they should be understood not through what they do, but by who they are.[1] Or we find the diaconate defined by clerical status in canon law, or by a sacramental character imprinted at ordination, or by a set of relationships to the Church and the faithful, or by a vocation to service. We often see the deacon in everyday circumstances, in dress or in action, as a kind of assistant priest. In the theological literature there is more rigor about definitions, but often the diaconate still comes across as a grab bag of miscellaneous attributes or is presented in a partial and distorted way.

This chapter offers an account of the diaconate that is full and coherent enough to be the basis for a sound understanding of diaconal identity—of who deacons are and what they are tasked to do. If we can get the "diaconal" part right, we can move with confidence to examine ministerial identity. Seen in full, the diaconate brings into a single Church office the entire bundle of ecclesial functions, relationships, and symbolic roles into which the deacon enters as a result of ordination.[2] Thus, the diaconate has three dimensions—functional, relational, and sacramental. These must be understood both individually and in an integral combination if we are to see the diaconate in full.

THE DIACONAL FUNCTIONS: ONE MINISTRY

The functional aspect of the diaconate has occasioned widespread confusion. It should be clear, given the "three tasks" framework of *Lumen Gentium* 29, that the Church gives deacons particular things to do. Deacons exercise the ministries of word, liturgy, and charity, and, if we follow the council texts here, also "administration" and indeed leadership of a kind, with limitations and under supervision.[3] We saw in chapter 4 how the ministries of charity and administration emerge, somewhat uneasily, from the clergy's third task, governance, and how they become distinctive for deacons. Many treatments of diaconal ministry stick to the "three task" framework, making the ministry of charity alone the third task. This leaves out any definite leadership function or makes it implicit. For example, the United States Conference of Catholic Bishops' 2005 document, *National Directory for the Formation, Ministry, and Life of Permanent Deacons*, calls the deacon a "guide" in the title to the section on the task of charity, but the activity of guiding is not mentioned in the text itself, which pictures the deacon as doing the acts of charity himself.[4]

Seeing deacons as leaders clearly has provoked some unease among both theologians and Church leaders. The continuing stress on servanthood, together with the relative silence about leadership, give evidence of this ambivalence. Pope Benedict XVI's 2009 move to amend Canon 1009 of the Code of Canon Law to exclude deacons from acting, as bishops and priests do, in the person of Christ the Head, is on one level a simple clarification: deacons do not preside at the Eucharist.[5] Still, the change does seem to imply stricter limits on diaconal leadership more generally. Nevertheless, in practice the exercise of the other tasks by someone holding an office in the Church must involve some form of leadership, if only in "guiding" volunteers among the faithful. Nor does the emphasis on humble service that is part of the model of Christ the servant preclude deacons acting as leaders. In the New Testament, it is precisely the leaders of the Church who are called upon to be servants of all (Mark 9:33–35 and parallels, 10:42–45; Matt 23:9–12; John 13:12–15). This is a way of envisioning leadership, not a

75

denial of its exercise. In substituting a deacon's "administration" for a bishop or priest's "governing," *Lumen Gentium* 29 simply expresses that a deacon's leadership has limits and stops short of full pastoral oversight. In the same way, the formula "not for priesthood but for ministry" makes clear that the office does not involve presiding at the eucharistic assembly.[6] Yet even when implicit or pictured as somehow combined with the ministry of charity, leadership within limits remains a deacon's task. William Ditewig has provided a good model for how this function should be exercised in his writings about "servant leadership" by deacons, drawing together the theological tradition with recent secular treatments of effective leadership.[7]

Once it is clear, in light of the council documents and the everyday practice of ministry, that leadership is a diaconal role, we can return to the usual "three-task" framework. This is not the place to explore in detail what constitutes each of the diaconal tasks.[8] The fundamental point is to avoid a narrowly functional understanding of the tasks and to allow for the wide variety of ways in which they can be expressed and practiced in a deacon's ministry. The task of charity, a central function of deacons, must not be constricted into a list of activities such as serving in soup kitchens and homeless shelters, ministry in prisons and hospitals, visiting the sick and homebound, and similar "charitable work" as commonly understood. The charitable task includes the often-invisible encounters that a deacon has with persons who are suffering, needy, or marginalized in a wide variety of contexts; and also activities aimed at promoting social justice. Likewise, the task called "liturgy" goes beyond a deacon's formal roles: at Mass, in the sacraments of baptism and matrimony, in funerals or communion services, or in leading prayers and devotions of various kinds. This task really incorporates private prayer, the practice of the Liturgy of the Hours, and finally whatever in a deacon's way of being and acting may make God's presence known and praised in everyday life. In the same way, ministry of the word goes beyond preaching, proclaiming the gospel, or teaching RCIA and religious education to incorporate evangelization in the broadest sense.

But it is the totality of the tasks, not any individual one, that makes them characteristic of a deacon. There is not a single aspect of any one of them that can only be performed by a deacon, and that thus could serve as a functional marker for the diaconate. Any of them could be exercised by a priest or bishop. Most of them—certainly all the works of charity, along with evangelization and bringing holiness into everyday life—are straightforward expressions of Christian discipleship to which all the faithful are called. What makes any or all of them diaconal is the fact that they are incorporated together into a single Church office. And as a Church office the diaconate only makes sense if it is dedicated to exercising the totality of its functions. Indeed, the only reason to combine them in a single office is that the sum is greater than the parts. The tasks become diaconal when the ones not being practiced at a particular moment are at least implicit because they are performed by someone publicly committed to doing them all. Thus when a deacon is engaged in acts of charity or evangelization, these tasks are connected to the deacon's public role in the Eucharist and to his permanent commitment to the Church's life of prayer. The task of sharing the word is present, if not explicit, when the deacon is exercising any other ministry, and even in his life in the broader society, if only because he is witnessing to the faith by being publicly and permanently identified with the office of deacon. The emphasis on charity framed by *Lumen Gentium* 29 and developed in subsequent Church documents is a distinctive task for deacons only if it issues from and is marked by the diaconal roles in worship and in proclamation of the word.

As we saw in chapter 2, the foundational model for this integral ministry of word, liturgy, and charity is that of the apostles after Pentecost, recounted in Acts 2—6. The apostles brought the Seven into this one ministry, with a focus on the third task—immediately, service to the Hellenist widows. Because care for the needy was integrated with prayer and preaching in the ministry of the apostles, the immediate charitable task of the Seven took on a greater significance than mere help and kindness: their ministry to the widows became, in imitation of Jesus's own ministry to the suffering and marginalized, a present sign of the spread of God's kingdom. The three functions assigned to deacons as an integrated totality in *Lumen Gentium* 29 are, in fact, the original apostolic tasks of preaching, community prayer, and care for the needy. It is only after the Church grew that governing, and the pastoral task generally, became part of the apostolic ministry, eventually invested in bishops as community overseers. The charitable task never ceased to be part of the apostolic ministry, but the revival of the diaconate at Vatican II explicitly restored that task to the clergy.

Of course, in practical ministry not every deacon can be dedicated in an integral way to all three tasks with a special focus on charity. Individual deacons find their ministry weighted more in some areas than others, depending on need and talent.[9] Certainly, not all deacons can or should have formal ministry assignments that include significant commitments to all three tasks, with a focus in what is commonly understood as the ministry of charity. But the incorporation of the three tasks into a single ministry is a nonnegotiable baseline for a true understanding and practice of the diaconate. If this baseline is allowed to slip away, the result is a functional breakdown: we have only minipriests, or social workers, or catechists who happen to be ordained. Such a situation is incoherent as a theology of ministry; it is a loss to the Church; and it is a source of confusion and stress for deacons themselves, who find themselves without an intelligible identity or mission.

Like others who exercise offices in the church, deacons are not wholly defined by their functions. But who they are cannot be wholly separated from what they are tasked to do. The functional dimension, then, is an integral part of diaconal identity, the subject of this book. If we define that identity without reference to any set of functions, as a number of theologians have tried to do, we miss both the distinctive quality and the concrete content of the office. The diaconate then might be understood merely as a participation in the bishop's ministry of pastoral oversight, where the deacon takes on whatever functions are required to further that ministry in the local church.[10] Or a deacon's task could be defined as carrying whatever the Church's mission may be in a particular area into mainly nonchurch settings.[11] It is true that the ministries of both priests and deacons participate in the ministry of the bishop, who exercises the apostolic ministry in its fullness.[12] It is also true that diaconal ministry has a quality of flexibility, which a bishop (in practice, often a parish priest in consultation with the deacon himself) fits to the needs of the local church in a variety of ways. Nevertheless, diaconal office does come with a particular set of tasks, and so cannot be reduced to some unspecified participation in the bishop's ministry.[13] Nor can we define the diaconate solely by its individual tasks: this leads to the functional breakdown just described. Rather, the diaconate becomes distinctive and intelligible only when ordered to the totality of its tasks, and is further defined through its relational and sacramental dimensions.

THE RELATIONAL DIMENSION

Richard Gaillardetz has written of ministry as "ecclesial re-positioning," an apt formulation that reflects how any ministerial office places the holder in a set of definite relations within the Church different from those she or he had before, as a Christian disciple positioned through baptism and confirmation.[14] This way of understanding office captures what is distinctive about different kinds of ministries that are stable and defined enough to have a recognizable place in the institutional Church, whether through commissioning, election, employment, or ordination. By dint of becoming an abbot, a pastoral associate, a director of faith formation, a chaplain, a Catholic school principal, or a bishop, the holder of the office is put in a particular set of relations with the Church and with the community. If the ecclesial repositioning is commissioned through ordination, then the set of relations becomes public, permanent, and sacramental.

This relational dimension is evident already in the texts from the New Testament and the early Church that we examined in chapter 2. The deacon of 1 Timothy 3:8–13, who has a stable ministry of assistance in the local Christian community, is placed in a close collaborative relation to the overseer of that community. In Acts 6:1–6, which offers a model for what the diaconate later became, the Seven come into a new relation with the apostles who commission them, with the Hellenist widows whom they serve, and with the broader Jerusalem community that chooses them. Ignatius of Antioch strengthens this relational character for deacons further, making them integral members of a three-part ministry with bishops and elders/presbyters.

In the contemporary situation of a deacon, the defining relations are easy to pinpoint. The deacon is related to the bishop by a promise of obedience, and to a particular place (typically a diocese) by the canonical condition of incardination, which gives him the faculties to perform diaconal tasks in that area. More broadly, the deacon is related to the Church, whose life and mission he makes a permanent and public commitment to serve. Deacons typically have assignments that involve nonpermanent commitments as well, such as to a parish, diocesan program, charitable organization, hospital, or prison.

But it is the permanent and public set of relations within the Church that defines diaconal office as such. Deacons are differently positioned from bishops, who have a ministry of oversight and a role in the governance of the universal Church; and deacons differ from priests, who have a presiding, priestly, and often pastoral role with respect to particular communities of the faithful. The permanent and public character of the deacon's position, resulting from ordination, also makes his ministry different in kind from the offices held by the nonordained faithful, no matter how significant, longstanding, and responsible their ministries in the Church may be.[15]

For a deacon, the totality of these defining relations, because they are a permanent condition of his life and action, become constitutive of who he is as a minister in the Church. In this sense they provide the outlines of what traditional theological formulations would term an ontology for the diaconate, a way of framing how the deacon "is" permanently different as a result of having this office in the Church. Indeed, we can speak more usefully of a relational ontology and avoid entering into speculations about whether or how the officeholder, in himself, enters into some different state of being from those who are not ordained.[16] This relational ontology can also be found in marriage, through which each person in the couple, permanently and publicly, takes on a new, relationally defined identity as a spouse. By looking at a deacon's inner and outer being in this relational way, we can sidestep a static view of the officeholder in favor of a more dynamic view of the person-in-relationship. That dynamism translates into a question that is enriching for the practice of ministry and for a deacon's spirituality, too: How can the set of permanent relationships that began with ordination be deepened and strengthened to serve more fully the mission of the Church? The relational dimension of diaconal ministry, then, has an open-ended challenge that parallels the flexible and expansive character of a deacon's tasks.

THE SACRAMENTAL DIMENSION

The diaconate is sacramental in two senses, one arising from its grounding in the specific sacrament of holy orders, the other springing from the capacity of this office to represent some aspect of the divine mystery for the Church and to the world. These two senses of sacramentality are interconnected, and the second arises from the first.

As one of the Church's sacraments, ordination repositions deacons within the Church and specifically brings them into one of the three orders of the clergy along with bishops and priests. The rite and the order define the functional dimension of the office—specifically the "three-task" framework with a center of gravity in the ministry of charity—and also its relational aspect, the obedience to the bishop, and the service to the people of God and to the Church's mission.[17] The sacramental commissioning also means that the conferral of office is public and permanent, characteristics that undergird and strengthen the capacity of the office to represent a particular dimension of the divine mystery. The sacrament of orders explicitly involves, through the action of the Holy Spirit, a bestowal of grace to direct and strengthen the deacon's ministry.[18]

Since Christ also acts through the sacraments of the Church, we can say that Christ enables the one being ordained to be conformed or configured to him in a new way.[19] We see this clearly in baptism, where the one baptized is configured to Christ as Priest, Prophet, and King, and so is enabled to become a Christian disciple. In holy orders, the one being ordained is configured to Christ in ways that are specific to the office—its tasks, its position in the Church, its distinct mission. (Of course, any action by Christ through the sacrament is an enabling action: the deacon responds in freedom and may, in a personal sense, reject the offer or accept it only partially). The next two chapters argue that deacons, because of the way their office is structured, are configured to Christ specifically through Christ's servant and threshold dimensions. That configuration is expressed, in our second, broadly sacramental sense, through the deacon's ministerial identity as icon of Christ the servant and minister of the threshold.

The specific configuration to Christ enabled by diaconal ordination is strongly rooted in the Church and attuned to the graces of the Holy Spirit. The configuration is not a narrowly individual identification of the deacon with Christ. Such an understanding can result, as Alphonse Borras warns, in a "burdensome *alter Christus* [another Christ] spirituality," or indeed in a kind of spiritual narcissim.[20] Of course an individual deacon, through the grace of ordination and through the faithful exercise of his office, can and indeed should come more deeply into personal communion with Christ. But the configuration enabled by holy orders is structured by an office in the Church, is mediated by the Church, and is rightly lived out in service to the Church and its mission. Moreover, any Christ-centered foundation of diaconal identity must be balanced by a deacon's recognition of, and cooperation with, the workings of the Holy Spirit in the Church and in the world. In particular, as we saw already in chapter 2, the diaconate as a Church office is designed to be a vehicle and a support for the charisms (spiritual gifts) poured out by the Spirit on the Christian community and indeed on the world.

The diaconal office structured by holy orders and the configuration to Christ that this sacrament enables provide the foundation for the deacon's broader sacramentality that builds upon and extends beyond the sacrament of holy orders itself. This sacramentality is seen already in the New Testament, and is developed more fully in later tradition.[21] The virtue and vice lists in 1 Timothy 3:1–13 call on deacons, along with the overseers who would later be known as bishops, to model key aspects of the Christian life for the broader community. Both Ignatius and Polycarp develop this exemplifying role further, urging deacons to model Christ in a way that points to Christ as servant of the Father. Ignatius makes the deacon a type (*typos*) or model of Christ in the way that the bishops should be a type or model of God the Father, and elders/presbyters of the apostles.[22] Ignatius is pointing to some but not all of the servant dimensions of Christ that will be explored in chapter 8; the deacon in the text of Ignatius serves both the bishop and the Church/the faithful.[23]

This type or model language can be used broadly. Bishops and priests and married couples are enabled to represent some aspect of Christ's presence in the world: as shepherd or priest, or through being an image of the marriage between Christ and the Church. The deacon is called to represent specifically the servant and threshold dimensions of Christ and the Church, as the next two chapters will make clear. At Vatican II, the quote from Polycarp at the end of the first paragraph of *Lumen Gentium* 29 placed this model of a servant Christ, however sketchily, in the broader context of a servant Church. The two complementary models of diaconal identity developed in this book, Christ the servant and minister of the threshold, are expressions of the diaconate's sacramentality in this broad sense.

This ministerial identity with its broadly sacramental dimension, though it builds upon a foundation within the sacrament of holy orders, does not claim, or need to claim, identity with any "character" imprinted on the one ordained through the rite itself.[24] Any such claim would be hard to argue in any case, given the difficulty of defining a specific content to "character," beyond the view that sacramental grace (in baptism, confirmation, and ordination) effects something permanent in the recipient, so that the sacrament is not repeatable.[25] In the case of ordination, the difficulty is magnified in various ways, not least because there is one sacrament conferred in separate rites for three distinct offices.[26] Thus, must there be a single character for all the offices, in order to safeguard the unity and integrity of holy orders, or can there be a particular one for each office?

Even if each office had a distinct character, we would still need a coherent definition of the character for the diaconate. Fortunately, no such definition is required for the theological account of diaconal identity developed in the next two chapters.

The language used for the sacramentality of the diaconate varies widely, and before proceeding to our discussion of the two models, it is necessary to seek as much precision in terminology as the subject will allow. The variety of terms is found in the ways deacons have been said to represent Christ the servant, the model of their ministerial identity that has been dominant since the council. In diocesan websites, handbooks, and popular books dealing with the diaconate, one often finds the bald statement that the deacon is somehow modeled on Christ the servant, but without any explanation of what this means. The theological literature, too, tends to treat the capacity of the office to be an example as something readily understood rather than as a topic for analysis and explanation.

But consider the confusing terminology. Up to this point we have stuck with the broad terms "exemplify," "represent," and "model," along with their related nouns, in referring to this phenomenon. But if we dive into the full range of theological and popular treatments that appeal to Christ the servant, we discover that the deacon with respect to this dimension of Christ's person and activity is said to be a "sign," a "sacramental sign," an "image" or an "icon"; the deacon is portrayed as "symbolizing," or "personifying"; and in another way of expressing this last idea, of acting "in the person of."[27]

This book will continue to use the general terms "example," "model," and "representative" in referring to both models of diaconal identity. Following what is now rather common usage, the deacon is also called here an "icon" of Christ the servant. This word has a range of meanings that overlap with the other terms for representation in the general sense that one thing points to another, but "icon" can be used with the specifically religious meaning of an image that mediates, however imperfectly, the presence of God or one of the saints to the receptive viewer. Accordingly, its use for the deacon's exemplifying capacity with respect to Christ seems appropriate. Moreover, the expression "icon of Christ the servant" has come into fairly general use for the diaconate, particularly since the use of this term in the *Basic Norms for the Formation of Permanent Deacons* in 1998.[28] The threshold model of ministry has the same capacity to represent an aspect of Christ and the Church—specifically the dimension of threshold, rather than servanthood. This will become clear in the next two chapters. However, since it is awkward to combine "icon" with "minister of the threshold," we will apply the specific term "icon" only to Christ the servant.

The other words used for the exemplifying capacity of a deacon's ministry will be avoided, either because they are roughly equivalent to the terms used here, or because they may have implications that go beyond what our account of diaconal identity needs to show.[29]

Seen in full, then, the diaconate combines three dimensions. From the standpoint of function, the office integrates the three tasks of word, liturgy, and charity, with a center of gravity in charity. Although formal ministry assignments do not and cannot always reflect clearly this integration and balance of tasks, the Church frames the office in these terms and challenges all deacons, and those who supervise them, to aim in this direction. The functions must be broadly defined and incorporate a role of leadership in the community. The tasks should be practiced so far as possible to build upon each other and point to each other, as we find in Jesus's ministry for the kingdom of God and in the original ministry of the apostles after Pentecost. The relational dimension puts the deacon in a permanent and public relation of obedience to the bishop and of service to the Church and its mission. The sacramental dimension of the diaconate includes the entrance into the clergy in a permanent and public commissioning, as well as the capacity and duty to model particular aspects of the divine mystery for the Christian community and for the broader world. The next three chapters will explore the two models that together provide the key to a deacon's ministerial identity, and they will show how these models provide guidance for the practice of ministry in the settings where deacons find themselves.

CHAPTER EIGHT

• • • • • •

DIACONAL IDENTITY I

Christ the Servant

We saw in earlier chapters that, beginning with Vatican II and continuing particularly into the early 2000s, the primary key to the ministerial identity of deacons, in Church documents, treatments aimed at a broad audience, and theological writing, has been the image of Christ the servant. The appeal to this vision of diaconal identity, however, has been weakened by a lack of specifics about both its conceptual definition and its concrete implications for ministry. Moreover, some theologians have aimed serious criticisms against this overall approach, as we noted at the end of chapter 6. Meanwhile, many diaconate directors, theologians, and homilists have gone on describing deacons as icons of Christ the servant without seeming to be aware of how controversial this idea has become.

This chapter presents a careful analysis of what the expression *Christ the servant* actually means and examines how it can be applied usefully, first to Christian discipleship generally, and then in a more specific and intense way to the office of deacon. The argument builds upon the account of diaconal office developed in the last chapter, as combining functional, relational, and sacramental dimensions, all of which turn out to be illuminated by this key image. The account of the deacon as icon of Christ the servant in this chapter has been fashioned to withstand the criticisms, which will be reviewed at the end of the chapter. The critics have been very helpful in challenging us to come to a clear understanding of how this image may or may not function as a key to diaconal identity. But their criticisms have not undermined the coherence and usefulness of the model of Christ the servant for the ministry of deacons.

"SERVANT" AS A WINDOW ON THE PERSON OF CHRIST

In examining a possible analogy between a scriptural image of Christ and a particular kind of Christian minister, the first step is to gain an adequate understanding of the image itself.[1] Looked at closely and in its fullness, the metaphor of Christ as servant is even richer in insights for theological reflection, spirituality, and practical ministry than first appears.

Christ as servant is one of several windows into the single person of Christ. This window offers a perspective both into his nature as God's Son and into his saving action in the world. Of course, *servant* is applied to Christ in a metaphorical sense. It is in human relations that we find real servants, and from here we may ask in what ways Christ could be understood as having the same or similar attributes as these human servants. Any use of the image, then, involves shuttling back and forth between human relations and the divine mystery. Other metaphors found in Scripture, such as *bridegroom*, *shepherd*, *priest*, and *head*, offer additional perspectives on the person of Christ. The servant metaphor, then, while theologically fruitful, is far from containing the mystery of Christ in its fullness.

The Old Testament is the source for a range of servant roles that the New Testament writers apply to Jesus, often developing further implications for those roles in the process. The basic "servant" idea is that he or she performs tasks for a superior. The Old Testament context for this may be slavery in the sense that the master owns the servant, but that is not necessarily the case. Moreover, the social position of the servant may be humble or highly respected, depending on the status of the master and the kind of service performed.[2] For example, the servant, perhaps legally a slave, who oversees a king's household and estates, is clearly in a very high social position, far above the lowly kitchen maid, who is also a servant and may happen to be legally free. As we will see in a moment, the understanding of Christ as a servant includes elements of both the exalted and the humble dimensions of servanthood in the Old Testament.

Two particular Old Testament conceptions of a servant, both of them already metaphorical, provide the background for the New Testament understanding of Christ as servant. First, kings, prophets, priests, and other persons in the Old Testament who carry out tasks on God's behalf are called servants of God, a designation that applies well to Christ in carrying out his mission in obedience to the Father. Second, the servant in Isaiah 40—55 is specially chosen by God and gives himself for the people of Israel, in particular by taking their sins upon himself and suffering pain and rejection.[3] Both of these concepts of servanthood are richly developed in the New Testament presentation of the way Jesus offers himself for the spread of God's kingdom and for the salvation of humankind. Those New Testament developments, taken together, are what constitute the metaphor of Christ the servant. A detailed investigation of the metaphor and its implications would take us far outside the scope of this book. Here we will sketch out the image of Christ the servant using an analytical method adapted from the procedure Avery Dulles uses in his treatment of the servant model of the Church.[4] By isolating the constituent parts of the image and looking at each in turn, we can construct a framework for applying the image to diaconal ministry with some clarity and rigor. The analysis also brings out the range of connotations in the servant/service complex of ideas when applied to Christ, and helps us to avoid focusing on only part of the image we are trying to understand.

FOUR ASPECTS OF CHRIST THE SERVANT

The image of Christ the servant combines four dimensions whose interconnections give it a unity of meaning. First, there is the question, "whose servant?" Considered as a servant serving a master, Christ does not his own will, but the will of the one who sent him. He is obedient to the Father, coming into the world to bring light into the darkness and to establish God's kingdom (Mark 14:36 and parallels; John 5:30; 6:38; 12:49–50).

Second, we have the question, "serving whom?" Christ gives himself to serve the needs of the world by offering salvation, forgiveness, and healing. Particularly in John's Gospel (13:1–17; 17:6–26), he ministers in an intimate way to his own community of disciples. In the larger world, Christ serves with special care the neediest and the victims of injustice—the poor, the outcast, the sick, and the disabled.

The third question is, "serving how?" Christ serves the Father's will, and serves the needs of the world, in a manner that is not dominating, but self-giving. He came not to be served, but to serve (Mark 10:42–45; Matt 20:25–28). It is a mode of humble service, as dramatically enacted in the foot-washing scene in John's Gospel (13:1–17), and as exemplified in Jesus's mingling with sinners and outcasts. Moreover, he came into the world as one of the powerless, without status or recognized authority, for example as a priest or a scribe. He was powerless even among a subject people, the Jews, who were themselves dominated by the Roman imperial system. In a further extension of this humble service, he gave himself for the salvation of the world by "taking the form of a slave," in the memorable formulation of the hymn in Paul's letter to the Philippians, and by undergoing a humiliating death understood by his followers through the lens of Isaiah's Servant Songs.[5]

Finally, we ask "what service" it is that Christ the servant offers. Christ's gift of self in humble service manifests itself especially in two areas of his salvific activity. One is to effect our redemption on the cross as the suffering servant. The other, seen in Jesus's ministry, is to offer healing and salvation, particularly to the poor and suffering (Luke 4:18–19; Matt 11:4–5). To those he encounters, Jesus addresses both their physical needs, such as healing and nourishment, and their existential needs—for hope, truth, solace in suffering, participation in community life, and salvation from sin and death. Jesus's works of charity are important in a this-worldly sense, intended to alleviate real physical and emotional suffering (Matt 25:34–40). But his service to the world is fundamentally a witness to the kingdom and a sign of God's presence; the works of charity flow from the proclamation of the kingdom and point to its consummation.[6]

FOUR ASPECTS, ONE SERVANT

The four aspects of Christ as servant just sketched converge into a single rounded image that makes theological sense. The following two series of interconnections illustrate the coherence. In serving the Father's will (#1, "whose servant?"), Christ expresses that will by serving the needs of a sinful and suffering world (#2, "serving whom?"), in the self-giving mode of a humble servant (#3, "serving how?"), and in this manner expressing God's particular solidarity in service to the poor and suffering (#4, "what service?"). Or, starting from a different direction, Christ's humble situation, his absence of status and power (#3, "serving how?"), reflect in worldly terms his complete submission to the will of the Father (#1, "whose servant?"); and represent the means by which the Father serves the needs of the world, especially the poor and suffering (#2, "serving whom?"), particularly through Christ's offer of healing and salvation (#4, "what service?"). The different aspects of this image of Christ, then, build upon each other and supplement each other to frame a single, intelligible window on the person of Christ, who is recognized in the self-emptying and self-giving love that undermines the logic of domination and presses forward in service to God's kingdom.

We noted in chapter 6 that this image of Christ the servant inspired one vision of the Church found in the documents of Vatican II, and we will see in a moment how Christ as servant provides a model for the ministry of deacons. But first it is important to note that this dimension of Christ is an example that guides every faithful Christian.

CHRIST THE SERVANT AS A MODEL OF CHRISTIAN DISCIPLESHIP

The envisioning of Christian discipleship through the lens of Christ the servant began already in the New Testament period, and this vision has remained a constituent element in the understanding and practice of Christian faith.[7] We can follow the analogy, with appropriate adjustments for the differences between Christ and human persons, through each of the four aspects of the servant image just analyzed. Thus, Christian disciples are to serve God's will in all things ("whose servant?"); to be humble, charitable, and self-giving with one another ("serving how?"); to proclaim the good news, and to be ministers of healing and reconciliation ("what service?"); to bring that good news to a sinful world, and especially to the poor and suffering ("serving whom?"). Thus, after moving upward by analogy from human social relations to gain insight into the servant dimension of Christ, we return downward by analogy from the theme of Christ as servant to flesh out the servant aspect of Christian discipleship.

If all Christians are called to model Christ the servant, how should this metaphor be applied specifically to diaconal ministry? We saw in chapter 5 that the application flowed from the twentieth-century ideal of a servant Church, and from the move at Vatican II to bring Christ the servant into the clergy itself by renewing the diaconate.

CHRIST THE SERVANT IN THE STRUCTURE OF DIACONAL OFFICE

The next step, then, is to see how diaconal office, as revived at Vatican II, is structured in a way that represents Christ the servant with a particular intensity. Since all Christian discipleship is modeled, in part at least, on this image of Christ, it follows that bishops, priests, and deacons, too, insofar as they practice authentic Christian faith, should be examples of Christ the servant. Moreover, as we saw in chapter 5, the council called on all the leaders of the Church, and in particular the Church's ordained ministers, to be servants of the people of God, in an understanding of servanthood that contains much of the metaphor of Christ the servant.[8] All Christians and indeed all Christian leaders, then, are called to model Christ the servant. But the diaconate, in its very structure and definition, is called to exemplify Christ the servant for the whole Christian community. Individual deacons do so more or less well in practice, of course. It is the office itself that holds out the model as a challenge to deacons and through them to the people of God as a whole.

To put some clarity and rigor into this claim, we will come at it from two directions. One starts from the model of Christ the servant, the other from the office of deacon. Thus, we begin by highlighting how each of the four aspects of Christ's servanthood, as presented earlier in this chapter, is expressed in the characteristics of diaconal office. Next, we turn to the office itself and examine how its functional, relational, and sacramental dimensions, examined in chapter 7, each contributes to the deacon's capacity to represent Christ the servant.

Like Christ in his servanthood, then, the deacon serves the will of another ("whose servant?"), always acting as the agent, the assistant, the one who is sent—particularly serving the bishop, but also priests in their role of standing in for the bishop in the local community. This aspect of servanthood is clearest in the deacon's role assisting the presider at the Eucharist, and in the practice of diaconal ministry assignments that are always subject to broader pastoral oversight.[9] The deacon serves with a completeness of subordination, of servanthood, that is unique among three grades of ordained ministry.

Like Christ, the deacon is the servant of all ("serving whom?"). Christ leads the disciples by acting as a servant, as seen most clearly in the foot-washing scene in John's Gospel (John 13:13–15). Deacons, like all ordained ministers, serve the people of God, but do so with a particular stress on servanthood because they are never, as deacons, in the presiding or oversight role within the community.[10] Christ's service to the world is expressed with particular clarity in the deacon's focus on works of charity and on witnessing for the Church in secular settings.

Like Christ, the deacon is called to be a humble servant, distanced from power or status ("serving how?")—particularly within the clergy, where he occupies the "lower level" with the most limited powers in both the sacramental and pastoral realms. And finally, like Christ the servant, the deacon is particularly tasked with a ministry of charity, in solidarity with the poor, the suffering, and the outcast ("what service?").

The distilled representation of Christ the servant just summarized grows out of the ecclesial relationships and responsibilities into which a deacon enters, permanently and publicly, as a result of ordination: circumscribed and supervised leadership; limited powers with respect to the clergy's three tasks to teach, sanctify, and govern; and an emphasis, within the three diaconal tasks, on humble and charitable service. The image of Christ the servant thus offers a distinctive key to the deacon's ecclesial identity, one qualitatively different from that of bishops and priests on the one hand and of all the baptized on the other.

The image is also rooted in each of the three aspects of diaconal office sketched in chapter 7. In the functional dimension, we see this in the focus on charity within an integrated exercise of all three diaconal tasks. Jesus's integration of works of this-worldly charity within a broader ministry of proclamation and symbolic action offers a particularly apt analogy for the stress on charitable service within the combined tasks of word, liturgy, and charity that together make up diaconal ministry.

The image of Christ the servant is also clear in the relational dimension of diaconal office, where the deacon always acts as the agent or assistant of the bishop or priest, and is in a serving relation both to the people of God and to the needs of a broader world. Finally, the sacramental dimension of diaconal ministry, the entrance into an order with permanent and public characteristics, is what provides the solidity that enables a deacon to do the representing of Christ the servant in the first place, however imperfectly real holders of this office actually do so.

If both the servant metaphor and the office of deacon are understood clearly, then a deacon in his ministry is indeed called to be an icon of Christ the servant—within the clergy, for the Church, and for the world. The age-old formula of Polycarp, colored by the vision of a servant Church in the quotation from Vatican II's *Lumen Gentium* 29, has developed into a theologically cogent model for diaconal ministry in the years since the council. This vision of diaconal identity also provides solid guidance for the practice of ministry, as chapter 10 will show. Once framed correctly, moreover, this model for the diaconate is not undermined by the criticisms that have been leveled against it.

THE CRITICS

Two general lines of argument have questioned the validity of Christ the servant as a model for diaconal identity. The first casts doubt on the theological coherence of applying this theme to the office or argues that the model has negative implications for ministerial practice. This book presents a detailed argument that comes to the opposite conclusion and incorporates responses to many of these criticisms, so the most significant critiques of this kind will be covered briefly here, referring back to positive arguments made already. The second line of criticism, developed by John N. Collins, argues that key components of Christ the servant as a model for the diaconate lack scriptural support, and, mainly for this reason, provide the wrong guidance for ministerial practice. His critique requires a fairly detailed treatment.

Within the first line of criticism, some have argued that since servanthood should be characteristic of all ministers, and indeed of all Christian disciples, this attribute cannot be distinctive for the diaconate.[11] But as we have just seen, diaconal office actually is structured to represent a particularly intensified image of Christ the servant; this in no way denies, but rather supports, the applicability of that model for other ministers and for the Christian faithful by offering a distilled version of it for all to see.

Richard Gaillardetz, starting from the emphasis on the mission of charity that is integral to both a deacon's ministerial identity and to Christ the servant, contends that this model points to a narrowly functional view of diaconal identity, envisioning the deacon as a sort of ordained social worker.[12] It is true that the task of charity is the center of gravity within the diaconal functions, but a correct understanding insists on the integration of this ministry into the full range of a deacon's tasks; places all three functions within the relational structure and sacramental framework of a deacon's office; and grounds the image of Christ the servant in all the dimensions of that office, not just in the charitable task. Moreover, as noted in chapter 7, the task of charity itself is not narrowly confined to functional assignments (such as "social work"), but incorporates a broad range of less formal encounters and situations that arise in diaconal ministry.

Finally, there is an undercurrent of unease among some critics with the "humble servant" aspect of this metaphor because it may undercut the appropriate exercise of leadership by deacons.[13] This is a real risk in practice, but as the analysis of diaconal office in chapter 7 notes, a correct understanding of the image of Christ the servant reveals it actually to be a model of leadership.

The second line of criticism, developed by John N. Collins, argues that this model for the diaconate should be rejected because it is based on a simple misunderstanding of words. The mistake came about, he says, through a wrong translation of the Greek term *diakonia* and the related *diakon-* words, widely used in early Christian writings, as denoting care and loving service. This misunderstanding arose in the Reformed Protestant tradition and directly influenced the modern development of a distinctly "diaconal" ministry focused on charitable service to the poor and suffering, particularly among German Protestants. Chapter 3 recounted the influence of this understanding of *Diakonie* on German Catholic proponents of a renewed diaconate in the years before the council. The mistranslation was given academic respectability by the New Testament scholar Wilhelm Brandt, himself a chaplain to German Protestant deaconesses, and then incorporated into the influential *Theological Dictionary of the New Testament* through entries on the *diakon-* words, authored by H. W. Beyer.[14] The German original of this work appeared in 1935.

In 1990, Collins published an exhaustive word study of the Greek *diakon-* words (including the noun *diakonos*, used for the office of deacon) in which he was able to show that "care, concern and love—those elements of meaning introduced into the interpretation of this word by Wilhelm Brandt—are just not part of their field of meaning."[15] Rather, the *diakon-* words point to situations in which one person acts as an agent or messenger for another, or performs in an assisting role. Further, there is nothing in the *diakon-* words themselves that suggests such actions should be seen as humble service. In a subsequent stream of books and articles, Collins has argued for an understanding of all ministry, including diaconal ministry, as being rooted not in any particular kind of service, but in the fact of being publicly commissioned and sent out on behalf of the Church.[16]

Collins's studies have demolished the basis of that (still) widely used word association that tends to equate diaconal ministry (*diakonia*) with humble, charitable service. Moreover, he has highlighted that the New Testament and early Church understanding of ministry, including its understanding of the office of deacon, provides no justification for envisioning the modern diaconate as especially devoted to humble service and works of charity.

However, these considerations, based as they are on the meanings of a certain word group in the New Testament and early Christian literature, do not actually define or even address the diaconate as revived at Vatican II.[17] In the first place, there is no reason why the character of diaconal office should be circumscribed by the original range of meaning for the *diakon-* words. This is true even of the ancient office, and much more so of the modern revival. Looking at the ancient diaconate, we find it is very probable that *diakonoi* received their titles because they acted as assistants of the overseers in early Christian communities, as we saw in chapter 2. However, the office of deacon did not originate with a clear focus on charitable service, and certainly not within the threefold ministry of word, liturgy, and charity that characterizes the revived diaconate of Vatican II.[18]

An official title may stay the same, while its content shifts and develops. Already in the ancient Church, the title of *presbyteroi*, or "elders," remained unchanged even while their ministry was increasingly understood through the lens of eucharistic presiding rather than age or mature judgment, as the original title suggests, until the office came to be understood as priesthood.

When the participants at Vatican II sought to adapt the structure of ministry to meet the challenges of their own time, they envisioned a development from the ancient office, and from the original sense of *diakonos*, aimed at extending the Church's pastoral reach and framed by the metaphor of Christ the servant. Such a move, far from cutting away the modern diaconate's roots in the New Testament, actually follows the pattern of ministry we find in the New Testament itself. As we noted in chapter 2, the early Christian communities developed a diversity of ministries in response to missionary and pastoral needs. Likewise, the council acknowledged the foundations of the diaconate in Scripture and in the early Church, but built upon them to adapt the structure of ministry to contemporary challenges. In doing this they followed the New Testament pattern, and their initiative moreover has been validated by subsequent pastoral results. In summary, while Collins's critique has been valuable in helping us to use our words more carefully, it lacks normative force for defining the ministerial identity of the revived diaconate or for evaluating the incorporation of Christ the servant into the understanding of this ministry. For a further analysis of problems with Collins's use of the "deacon words" to develop a model of diaconal identity, see appendix 3.

In subsequent work on the present-day diaconate appealing to early Christian models and considered from an ecumenical viewpoint, Collins is particularly concerned to avoid identifying the diaconate with "selfless loving service" as a specialized activity not fully rooted in the Christian community and its mission. This, he notes, was a common pattern for Protestant deaconesses dedicated to charitable work and living apart from local communities in motherhouses.[19] Collins does not deny that charitable service may be a special focus of diaconal ministry, but he insists on a fully ecclesial context for it. Thus, he argues that "an understanding of *diakonia* must be cultivated which embraces social welfare without simply being identified with it. One way to attempt this is through a sacred commission."[20] This would provide a recognizable role for diaconal ministry within the community, root that ministry in liturgy, and make clear that the deacon's service inside and beyond the community aims to "extend the benefits of the commemorative meal so far as they will reach."[21] In fact, the Roman Catholic permanent diaconate is structured on precisely this model: permanent commissioning through ordination; a recognizable office combining three tasks; rooted in word and liturgy, moving outward from them in the focus on charitable service. The scriptural image most foundational to this vision of the diaconate, moreover, is Christ the servant.

CONCLUSION

Widespread appeals to the image of Christ the servant, in Church documents, theological reflection, and popular presentations of the diaconate from Vatican II to the present, suggest that both deacons themselves, and those who form or direct them, have found this model to be enriching and useful. Critics, meanwhile, have pointed out potential distortions and misapplications that need to be taken seriously if this important key to diaconal self-understanding is to be salvaged. Taking up that challenge, this chapter has brought together four interconnected aspects of Christ as servant, and then applied the image in its fullness to the office of deacon. Subjected to this rigorous treatment, the model highlights the diaconate's separation from power in the Church, its humble style of ministry and leadership, and its focus on this-worldly charity within a broader ministry of word and sacrament. The model also gives theological weight to the diaconate's emphasis, in its pattern of relationships, on service: to the bishop, for the people, and for the Church's mission in the world. In these concrete ways, then, deacons are indeed called to be models or icons of Christ the servant.

CHAPTER NINE

• • • • • • •

DIACONAL IDENTITY II

Minister of the Threshold

The theological and pastoral conversation about the diaconate has suggested a second, complementary model of diaconal identity besides Christ the servant. The various suggestions pointing to this model have not been gathered into a single framework before, but they all express an integral dimension of the life and ministry of deacons that is not captured by the model of Christ the servant. Chapters 3 and 6 have touched on a number of the ideas about the diaconate that contributed to this second approach in writings before and after the council. These include the idea of the deacon as a bridge figure between the higher clergy and the laity, or between the Church and the world; deacons are seen as having a special capacity to fill this role as members of the clergy living in the same social conditions as the laity and as people outside the Church community entirely. Several more recent explorations of diaconal identity, particularly in Germany, have developed the idea of a bridge ministry in new directions, envisioning deacons as most characteristically practicing ministry in a "borderland between secularity and holiness," or as having a unique capacity to identify with the outcast or the "other."[1]

    This chapter presents that second model of diaconal identity as a ministry of the threshold. Like the model of Christ the servant, this understanding of the diaconate grows out of a theologically rich metaphor. A threshold, as a place of meeting and passage between different places or realities, suggests the ideas of bridge, borderland, and mediation that have contributed to this perspective on the deacon's ministerial identity over the decades. The threshold model is designed to bring together various strands in that conversation into an intelligible, unifying image that has as much theological weight and practical usefulness as Christ the servant.

Our examination of the threshold model generally will parallel the method followed for the treatment of Christ the servant. To give the image of ministry at the threshold a theological foundation, this model will be rooted, like the image of Christ the servant, in the person and activity of Christ. We will then look more closely at the image of a threshold both as a place and as a metaphor for particular realities in the Church and in the life of Christian discipleship. Next, the threshold model will be applied to the office of deacon: first, as an intensification of the threshold aspect of all Christian discipleship; then as an integral element in the deacon's office with its functional, relational, and sacramental dimensions. This analysis shows how the office itself is uniquely structured and positioned in the Church to be a ministry of the threshold. Further, we will be able to note several strengths this model has both for understanding a deacon's distinct ministry and for complementing the theme of Christ the servant in developing a full picture of diaconal identity.

In certain respects, the view of diaconal identity as a ministry of the threshold has different characteristics than the model of Christ the servant, which has been the basis of most reflection about the ministry of deacons since the council. The threshold idea has not been proposed in a single framework with interrelated aspects before. Nor have the perspectives from various writers that contribute to it, either individually or collectively, gained enough prominence to provoke a debate, along with the helpful challenge of critical scrutiny. The threshold model of diaconal identity does not have much explicit support in Church documents, where the model of Christ the servant is dominant. In addition, the threshold idea depends more importantly on the context in which diaconal ministry is practiced, and therefore may be more subject to adjustment as that context changes. This chapter and the next show that the threshold idea has a strong theological grounding, applies usefully to a deacon's ministry, and complements that of Christ the servant for providing a full account of diaconal identity. Chapter 11 will consider how the model might be applied amid possible changes in the typical context of diaconal ministry.

THRESHOLD AS PLACE AND METAPHOR

To begin an examination of ministry at the threshold, imagine yourself standing in a doorway looking at what is under your feet. The threshold is the lower sill of the doorway, and it must be crossed to enter or leave the building. When you cross the threshold, you move from one place to another, from inside to outside or vice versa. If you stand on the threshold, you are between two places, at the outer limit of each. The threshold, then, is both a particular kind of in-between place, when considered statically, and a marker for movement, when you are going across it from one place to another. More generally, the threshold is an image for any border, edge, frontier, margin, or limit between different realities.[2]

CHRIST AS A THRESHOLD FIGURE

The person and mission of Christ exhibit a strong character of being at or crossing a threshold, primarily in a metaphorical sense, but even in the sense of moving through physical and geographical space. This character has multiple aspects; five are offered here as illustrations. The five aspects may not exhaust all the possibilities of looking at Christ as a threshold figure, but they present a picture that is full enough to be applied usefully to ministry. Like the image of Christ the servant, the threshold metaphor offers one window on the person and activity of Christ. The image of a threshold is fully grounded in the Christ of Scripture, although the scriptural texts do not explicitly apply the threshold image to Christ as they do with the servant metaphor.

First, within Israel the mission of Jesus has a two-way movement, both in and out, across social thresholds. The ingoing movement is also geographical: the journey from the cultural and religious margins in Galilee to the center of Israel's life and worship in Jerusalem.[3] We can imagine the crossing of this threshold as Jesus's entry into Jerusalem on Palm Sunday, when he comes into both Israel's holy city and into the events of his passion, death, and resurrection. The second movement is outward: the mission of Jesus is especially aimed at the margins of the people of Israel, to those without status or power, those who are not fully included at the center of the community: to the poor, the sick, the lepers, the unclean, the blind, and the lame; to sinners, and in general to the "lost sheep of the house of Israel" (Matt 10:5–6; 15:24).[4] The mission of Jesus also goes out to and includes women in a way that crosses over an important threshold between gender-based social spheres and roles in his time (Mark 5:25–44; John 4:1–27; Luke 10:38–42).

Second, the ministry of Jesus takes him across a boundary threshold to strangers just beyond Israel: to the Syrophoenician woman and the Samaritan woman, who live in lands bordering Israel (Mark 7:24–30; John 4:5–30); and to non-Jews resident in Israel but not part of the people, such as the Roman centurion (Matt 8:5–13).

Third, as "light to the nations," Christ in his mission passes boldly over the outer threshold of Israel to the world beyond. This happens after he crosses over another threshold, that of death, and returns in the resurrection, giving his apostles the great commission to go out and baptize all nations (Matt 28:19; 24:14). They and their followers would do so after his ascension under the guidance of the Spirit (Acts 2:1–12; 15:22–35).

Fourth, as we see particularly in John's Gospel, Christ passes twice over the threshold of human life: he is sent out by the Father and then returns to the Father.[5]

Finally, we can see a threshold dimension in Jesus's proclamation of God's kingdom. This new reality has begun to be actualized in Jesus's own presence, but its fulfillment lies in the future at the end of the age. Jesus stands on the threshold of a new reality and invites his followers to cross that threshold with him.[6]

These threshold aspects of the person and activity of Christ are reflected in a deacon's ministry of the threshold, but as with the model of Christ the servant, the reflection is mediated through the deacon's position in the Church. In order to give an account of this mediation, we consider next how the Church itself becomes the vehicle for these threshold dimensions of Christ.

THRESHOLD AND CHURCH

We can begin by imagining an actual church building that has a threshold in the doorway separating the inside from the outside. But because in a metaphorical sense the Church is the Body of Christ, the threshold aspects of Christ's person and activity just illustrated have parallels in the Church as a spiritual and human reality. These parallels, once understood, will help us to locate a Church ministry for deacons within the threshold dimensions of the Church itself. There are three kinds of ecclesial thresholds: within the Church, between the Church and the wider world, and in the reality that the Church and its faithful live out.

First, there is a threshold-crossing reality inside the church building that parallels the mission of Christ within Israel. In the liturgical assembly we find an actual threshold between the sanctuary and the worshipers. This is clearest in the Eastern Rite and Orthodox Churches, where an icon screen with doors separates the two areas, but it is still the case in a Western context, even if the sanctuary extends into and is surrounded by pews, as is the style for many contemporary buildings. The eucharistic sacrifice is centered in the sanctuary, and there is movement into it (procession[s] in, gifts) and movement out (distribution of communion, procession out.) These parallel the two-way movement of Christ within Israel: into the center at Jerusalem for the enactment of the paschal mystery, and outward in the ministry of proclamation, healing, and conversion. The qualification, of course, is that the worshipers are not the marginalized, the second-class citizens, to whom Jesus particularly aimed his mission. They are the people of God at prayer. But the gifts of word and Eucharist that move out across the sanctuary threshold are offered especially to those most broken and needy among them.

Second, the threshold of a church's doorway is an image marking another dual movement: out from the eucharistic community to the broader world and back from the world into the eucharistic assembly. These movements across the Church's threshold are central to the Church's mission in the world and reflect all three of the next threshold dimensions of Christ we just identified. For the Church as a spiritual and human reality, the outward movement is the mission of evangelization, with all that this implies, from the proclamation of the truth to the sharing of divine blessings and the medicine of mercy. The return movement is the invitation and gathering of the world's people into a new reality, into God's own life, and into God's kingdom of love and justice, for which the Church is tasked to be Christ's special vehicle. As the Church and the world go on in the present age, of course, neither movement is completed: the Church still has a recognizable "inside" and "outside." These outgoing and incoming movements in the life of the Church reflect the second, third, and fourth threshold dimensions of Christ illustrated a moment ago. Christ's mission moved out from Israel, first to the resident stranger and to the borderlands, then to the nations. That mission invited those outside to come into a new Israel, God's kingdom. And Christ undertook this mission by going out from the Father and returning to the Father.

Third, the Church and its faithful live in a threshold place. We are between spiritual and temporal dimensions, between an origin and final home in the divine mystery on the one hand, and human existence, with its particular physical, moral, and social horizons, on the other. The threshold place where Christ's disciples and his pilgrim Church live, moreover, parallels the fifth and final threshold dimension of Christ touched on above, the inbreaking but as yet unfulfilled reality of God's kingdom.

These brief reflections on the threshold dimension of the Church could be elaborated considerably, but this sketch should be enough to allow us to draw out some implications for ministry. But before doing so, it is important to note that there is a threshold dimension to all Christian discipleship, a dimension that mirrors this aspect of the Church.

CHRISTIAN DISCIPLESHIP AT THE THRESHOLD

Within the church building and its gathered community, the movement back and forth across the sanctuary threshold for the faithful is mainly metaphorical rather than spatial: the worshipers pray toward the sanctuary as they participate in the Eucharist; they then carry within themselves the spiritual reality of the Eucharist in their mission to share in building up the Body of Christ through participating in community life. In the movement back and forth between the Church and the broader world, all Christian disciples are called to cross the Church threshold to participate in the mission of evangelization. In a return movement back across the threshold, the faithful are called to aid in gathering the peoples into God's kingdom of love and justice, and into fellowship in the Church. Finally, all Christians are called to live faithfully in this threshold place of human joys and sorrows, temptations and limits, framed by an origin and destiny in God.

This brief sketch of the threshold dimensions of Christian discipleship shows that discipleship to be a challenging calling, a goal that actual Christian disciples and their local church communities frankly may honor more in the breach than in the observance. In particular, the Catholic faithful, unlike many evangelicals, often do not understand evangelization as a core calling of the life of faith, assuming instead that this task will be handled by clergy or specially trained missionaries or members of religious orders. But it is important to see the goal of all Christian discipleship clearly, especially here in an examination of ministry. The task of ministers is not to take on this goal of full discipleship as a specialized one for themselves. Their task, rather, is to support and animate the people of God in stretching toward it.

DIACONAL MINISTRY AT THE THRESHOLD OF THE CHURCH

In each of the threshold dimensions of the Church, the office of deacon brings something more structured and intense to the universal call of Christian discipleship. Within the church itself, this begins in the Mass, as deacons are characteristically at or moving across the sanctuary threshold, sometimes physically, at other times by speaking. Yves Congar noted this in his 1965 article, discussed briefly in chapter 6, where he envisioned the deacon as a bridge minister by reflecting from a starting point in this aspect of liturgy. These diaconal roles are far clearer in the Eastern Rites, where deacons move back and forth through "deacon doors" in the icon screen at the threshold of the sanctuary. Yet we can find them in contemporary Western rites, if less distinctly expressed. Besides processing into and out of the sanctuary with the celebrant, deacons proclaim the Gospel from the sanctuary outward to the people; by praying the penitential rite and intercessions, they bring the prayers of the people into the sanctuary; deacons receive the gifts at the sanctuary threshold and prepare the table; and back at the sanctuary threshold they distribute the cup. In the absence of a deacon, of course, celebrants or extraordinary ministers perform all these functions; but when deacons are present and do them, the liturgy is enriched by a more dynamic interplay between the priestly aspect of the Eucharistic sacrifice and the worshiping community. In this liturgical context, at least, it is appropriate to speak of the diaconate as an "intermediate order" between the priest or bishop and the faithful.

This liturgical movement in action and speech across the sanctuary threshold is mirrored in the everyday conditions where a deacon's ministry is practiced within the local church community. The people in the pews see deacons whose lives resemble their own (typically including marriage, family, work, and the various ordinary participations in social life), but who are publicly and permanently committed to serve the mission of the Church, not just in liturgical and pastoral roles, but wherever they find themselves. This may be in the workplace, on the sports field, in the school or civic meeting, at the store or the gym, in all kinds of social or familial gatherings. To these encounters the deacon brings not only the mission of Christian discipleship, but also a distinctive ecclesial presence flowing from ordination with its lifelong public commitment. Even when doing ministry in a Church setting, deacons are, as one pre-Vatican II author aptly envisioned, "canonically of the clergy, but sociologically of the laity."[7] This threshold place has rich possibilities for building up the Body of Christ, possibilities that are distinct from those available to priests and bishops on the one hand, and to all the faithful on the other. Deacons can integrate this everyday "lay" experience into preaching and into the way they carry out formal ministry assignments, from baptism and marriage preparation to prayer groups or adult faith formation. They also have broader opportunities than bishops and priests for encountering and accompanying the faithful in both the locations and the existential realities where they live.

It is in crossing the Church threshold into the broader world that diaconal ministry is at its most characteristic. Like all the people of God, the deacon is tasked with bringing the good news to a broken and often uncomprehending world, and of inviting people everywhere, through faith and inner conversion, to participate in God's banquet. But for the deacon this calling is intensified, precisely because he is an ordained minister embedded in the world outside the Church. And because ordination is public and permanent, the deacon is called upon to express, in speech and action, not only his Christian discipleship, but his identity as one permanently committed to a distinct ministry in the Church's mission. The expression of this call can take many forms, of course, and it must be practiced with prudence and discernment as well as boldness. But the condition itself, that of being a member of the Catholic clergy embedded in the broader world, is a threshold place that is distinctive for deacons. Some practical implications of this aspect of diaconal identity will be discussed in the next chapter.

Finally, deacons live a particularly intensified form of the threshold existence between the spiritual and temporal dimensions that characterizes all Christian discipleship. If a deacon takes seriously the public character of his commitment to the Church and participation in the order of deacons, then the tension between these commitments and his activities in the world must become greater. And this inner tension, this stretching to go beyond a routine and conventional way of living in the world, will become recognizable to others in the everyday interactions of workplace, family, and society, as well as in formal ministry assignments. Others may glimpse, for example, some elements of the personal sacrifices and inner redirection that accompany the deacon's permanent commitment to serve the Church; or they may recognize that the deacon's daily interactions are somehow rooted in prayer and liturgy; or they may see that for the deacon the witness to core truths and values of the Church is nonnegotiable, even while the deacon is fully engaged in secular activities. Through an intensification of the threshold existence of Christian discipleship, then, diaconal office calls upon the deacon to exemplify that existence in the world with particular clarity and faithfulness.

THRESHOLD MINISTRY IN THE THREE DIMENSIONS OF THE DIACONATE

The threshold model of diaconal ministry becomes even clearer when we examine how it illuminates each of the three dimensions— functional, relational, and sacramental—of a deacon's office. As we saw in chapter 7, the functional aspect of diaconal ministry calls for the integral practice of the three tasks of word, liturgy, and charity, with a center of gravity in charity. This grounding in the ministry of charity draws the deacon particularly to those at the margins, both within the Church community and outside it. Acts 6 provides the model: the apostles, whose threefold ministry of proclamation, prayer, and charity needs extension to those at the margins who are being over-looked (the Hellenist widows), commission the Seven to serve the widows' needs. Through the commissioning, this immediate act of charity expresses as its motivation and ultimate purpose the fullness of the Spirit-led evangelization incorporating proc-lamation and prayer. Likewise, diaconal ministry, through the grounding in charity, is specially aimed at those in the Church community who are at the margins: the overlooked, the for-gotten, the alienated, those who suffer in silence, or those who because of age or sickness cannot join the community at the eucharistic table. Of course, this does not mean that deacons can or should avoid collaboration with the active faithful, the leaders, those who have made or can make significant contri-butions to community life. But for a minister of the threshold there is always a pull toward the edges, modeled on the thresh-old dimension of Christ, whose mission was especially aimed at those at the social margins or on the boundaries of the people of Israel. The leadership function of diaconal ministry follows this movement to the edges as well, focusing particularly on animat-ing others within the Christian community to seek out and care for those at the margins.

In his role as an ordained minister embedded in the wider world, a deacon's three integral tasks with an emphasis on char-ity also point him particularly to those at the Church's outer frontier, and even beyond that: for example, to those who are estranged from or hostile to the Church; to the indifferent and the drifting; or to those whose suffering has vanquished hope in any reality beyond the horizon of human drudgery. The forms such encounters take will vary widely, but a characteristically diaconal approach begins in charity, in clearly willing the good of another as a person with real physical, existential, and spiritual needs. As in the healing ministry of Jesus, this charity, when practiced in an integral and publicly expressed mission that incorporates word and is rooted in prayer, carries within it the fullness of the gospel and an invitation into the new life in Christ. In actual situations, this fullness may hardly be glimpsed by others, but for charity to be an expression of diaconal min-istry, all three tasks, with their invitation to new life, must be at least implicit in the deacon's manner and action. When this occurs, an invitation is issued; thus it is no surprise that people in everyday contexts approach deacons seeking blessings, prayers, advice, help, or accompaniment in suffering. Some, too, sensing that the deacon's invitation is explicitly rooted in the Church, aim their critiques or resentments against the Church at the deacon. What kind of encounter happens depends on the context and on the deacon's particular mode of living diaconal identity. But since these encounters are taking place because the deacon is a recognizably ecclesial presence in the world, we can speak metaphorically of them as interactions happening on the Church's threshold. In another metaphorical sense, the deacon comes into these situations by crossing the Church's threshold and becoming embedded in the world beyond. In both these ways, then, deacons in their functional dimension express their identity as ministers of the threshold.

The key relational aspect of the diaconate as a ministry of the threshold is the deacon's relation to the Church itself. Through ordination this relation of service becomes permanent and public. In this sense the relation is analogous to marriage, which conditions the way the spouses live, not just when they are together, but when they are apart: each wears openly the promise of fidelity, expressing a certain nonavailability and rootedness elsewhere. So it is with the deacon's relation to the Church as he lives and practices ministry outside the formal confines of Church life: the relation conditions everything. It is through this permanent relation that the deacon becomes a member of the Catholic clergy embedded in the wider world, with all the possibilities for a ministry at the threshold that have been discussed already.

The permanence and stability of the deacon's relation to the Church is also, like the marriage relation blessed by the Church, sacramental. This is true in the narrow sense that the deacon's relation to the Church is rooted in the sacrament of holy orders. But it is also true in the broader sense that diaconal office, like the married state, has the capacity to represent some aspect of the divine mystery. A traditional understanding of this sacramentality for marriage is the spousal relation between

Christ and the Church. As a minister of the threshold, the deacon rightly exercising his office represents, for the Church, the threshold dimension of Christ's person and activity sketched above: the mission to those at the margins, the movement across the community's social thresholds with the invitation into God's kingdom, the inhabiting of a tensive place between divine and human, spiritual and temporal realities.

Diaconal ministry, then, mirrors the threshold aspects of Christ in the functional, relational, and sacramental dimensions of the office. The parallels are mediated through the position of diaconal office in the Church, which, as we have seen, has its own threshold dimension—within the church building and local community, across the Church threshold, and in the Church's spiritual/temporal existence. These aspects of the Church find distinct expression in the ministry of deacons, an expression that intensifies the threshold aspect of Christian discipleship and differs in its character and ministerial possibilities from the ministry of bishops and priests.

CONTRIBUTIONS OF THE THRESHOLD MODEL TO UNDERSTANDING DIACONAL IDENTITY

This vision of the diaconate as a ministry of the threshold extends and complements the model of Christ the servant in four key respects. First, the threshold model takes account of the everyday reality of diaconal ministry in ways that are not captured by the image of Christ the servant. In particular, the threshold model reflects a deacon's movement, through speech and action, into and out of the sanctuary, bringing dynamism to the interaction between worshipers and celebrant; the pull of diaconal ministry to those at the margins of the Church, both inside and outside the ecclesial community; the experience and ministerial possibilities of being an ordained minister embedded in the world, sharing the social life both of the Christian faithful and of those outside the Church; and the capacity to represent in a broadly sacramental way, both in the church and outside it, the threshold dimension of Christ, in their movement across social and institutional thresholds, sharing the good news and inviting all into a fuller life with God.

Second, the threshold model has enough independent theological weight to justify a separate formulation of diaconal identity to stand beside the image of Christ the servant. The model of the deacon as minister of the threshold is rooted in the person and activity of Christ, in the threshold character of the Church, and in the structure of diaconal office itself, not merely in the personal qualities or formal assignments of deacons in particular times and places.

Third, within the ongoing theological and pastoral conversation about diaconal identity, the threshold model can function both as a unifier and as a springboard for further reflection. As we have seen, this vision brings together several hitherto unconnected but important strands of thought about the diaconate going back decades: the idea of the deacon as a bridge minister, as occupying an intermediate place between the higher clergy and the laity, as having a distinct ministry aimed at the world beyond the currently gathered Church, as ministering from a borderland social location, and so on. The threshold image provides a common framework for such explorations, gives them necessary theological grounding, and places them in a relationship of complementarity with the dominant model of Christ the servant. Looking to the future, the threshold metaphor is open-ended and allusive enough to encourage further reflection about this aspect of diaconal identity.

Finally, the threshold model provides a dynamic vision of diaconal identity that captures a sense of mission and journeying, of ministry on the edge of something new that may be happening in or through the Church. Henri Denis expressed this succinctly already in 1965 when he envisioned the diaconate of the future as "the sign, in the world, of a Church in the making by God's grace," distinct from the Church already gathered under the leadership of bishops and priests.[8] This dynamic aspect of diaconal ministry is not a strong feature in the model of Christ the servant. That image envisions the diaconate in a more static way, placing deacons in a distinct ministry of service within the

Church ministries, providing a theological underpinning for the diaconal tasks with a focus on charity, and holding out the picture of a humble servant to guide a deacon's inner attitude and outer self-presentation. The threshold model, by contrast, relies mainly on images of motion—out, across, returning. It is true that the model of Christ the servant incorporates movement in the "sent-out" quality of the servant. And the threshold model includes the more static image of the intensified "in-between" existence of a deacon (spiritual/temporal, Church/world), pictured as standing at the threshold between the Church and the world outside. But the dominant image of diaconal ministry in the threshold model is of dynamic activity, of moving, of becoming. Besides complementing the more static metaphor of Christ the servant, the threshold model's dynamism offers a guide to the practice of diaconal ministry that is particularly energizing and open to new possibilities. These practical implications will be explored further in the next chapter.

CHAPTER TEN

• • • • • •

THE MODELS AS GUIDES TO MINISTRY IN PRACTICE

The last two chapters delineated two complementary models for the ministerial identity of deacons, models that show who deacons are and what the Church calls them to do. The emphasis so far has been on theological coherence and on how each model illuminates the office of deacon itself. This chapter examines what light the two models shed on the practice of diaconal ministry. We begin here by defining more precisely the purpose of the models, clarifying the method used for applying them, and specifying the practical results that will be sought. Next, we review briefly the conditions in the Church, society, and culture that are the typical context for the ministry of deacons. These conditions provide the practical testing ground for the two models. Then the practical implications of each model are examined in detail, to show how they contribute to giving the diaconate a recognizably distinct role among the Church's ministries and how they can be used as guides for shaping a deacon's vocation and ministry.

THE MODELS AND THEIR PURPOSE

This book has referred to the two accounts of diaconal identity mainly as models, although other words such as *image*, *representative*, and *icon* have also been used as near synonyms in context. The term *model* is employed in many disciplines from the social sciences to finance to theology, not to mention in everyday speech, so it is important to be clear about its meaning here.

The models of Christ the servant and minister of the threshold are not primarily designed to describe a ministerial situation as it is: instead, they hold out a goal. Of course, they do have a descriptive function as well. There would be no point in appealing to the theme of Christ the servant if the deacon were not, in actual fact, in a serving position with respect to both a bishop and the people of God. Nor would it make any sense to envision the deacon as minister of the threshold unless—to take one of the starting points for this image of diaconal identity— deacons did in fact practice ministry from an in-between place incorporating both ecclesial and secular spheres. But the models are not merely descriptive. Thus one cannot point to a particular deacon, or even to a large number of deacons, and say, for example, "They really just act as priests' assistants around the parish, so these models don't apply to them." If that characterization of their ministry is accurate, our models do not describe these deacons as they are; instead, the models point the way toward a fuller and indeed, truly diaconal, ministry. The models suggest ways to extend, enrich, complement, or at least compensate for the incomplete character of a ministry situation like that one.

The models, then, express a calling, both for an individual deacon and for a church with diaconal ministers. In these models, the deacon is called to represent, so far as possible, what the models reveal about the mysteries of Christ and the Church. We see this exemplifying role for deacons already in the virtue and vice lists of 1 Timothy 3:8-13, and in the way Ignatius and Polycarp exhort deacons to be "types" of Christ. Moreover, if these models correctly express diaconal identity, the Church, for its part, is called to choose, form, ordain, assign, and support deacons in order that those deacons may be, so far as circumstances permit, icons of Christ the servant and ministers of the threshold. In this chapter we will point to some specific ways in which deacons are called to represent these mysteries in the Church and in the world today.

In their mode of expression, the two models are not tight constructs or lists of specific directives; instead, they are multifaceted, rich in allusions, and open ended. This is what allows them to be fruitful guides in the wide variety of ministry situations found in the everyday world. Of course, the models have an inner logic, as the previous two chapters have shown. But they are fruitful guides to practice primarily because they are rooted in the depths of the Christian mystery. Each model begins with a metaphor (servant or threshold) that offers a perspective on the person and activity of Christ, and then extends to a parallel dimension of the Church and of Christian discipleship. Only from this broad perspective is it possible to see how the office of deacon is uniquely structured to represent and to put into action each model of ministry.

In order to function as a vehicle for integrating multiple aspects of a deacon's ministerial identity, each model holds out an image that we can hold in our mind, remember, and appeal to in practical situations. The most concrete way of picturing Christ the servant is surely the image of Christ washing the feet of his disciples: in it we see clearly the quality of humble service that is also an example for leadership, the act of addressing physical needs in a manner that brings in symbolically the full implications of the gospel, and the self-giving of Christ in obedience to the Father. For the threshold, the most characteristic image is the door of a church building, suggesting the passage between Church and world, and the edge place where the deacon's special mission is located.

Finally, precisely in order to be broadly applicable, the models cannot be either overly abstract and general or too detailed and specific. We will not learn much that is useful for concrete decision-making in ministerial situations by appealing to a very general, undefined image of servanthood, or to an exemplary personal holiness. On the other hand, a detailed list of rules and directives, useful as they may be in particular conditions, cannot give adequate guidance in the wide variety of cases that spring up in practical ministry. Accordingly, the models developed here steer a middle course between what is general and what is detailed. For practical ministry, they offer a reliable yardstick for reflection and discernment, a goal against which to assess an actual situation or direction, some broad guidelines for an authentically diaconal ministry, and a means to make that ministry particularly distinctive and recognizable as diaconal in the context where it is practiced. These two models do not provide the only criteria to be used in decision-making in ministerial situations. Any application of the models must take account of other factors as well, including actual pastoral and mission needs and a deacon's own gifts, shortcomings, commitments, and well-being. But by providing a full, theologically grounded, and concrete account of a deacon's ministerial identity, the models do furnish guidelines for addressing everyday situations and problems.

APPLYING THE MODELS IN PRACTICAL SITUATIONS

The two models can be applied usefully to practical questions that arise in diaconal ministry in three ways that are distinct but interrelated. The sections covering each model below will show how they do this. First, the models, if followed by deacons in ministry, should make the office more distinct, recognizable, focused, and effective. Church leaders, all the faithful, and even those who encounter deacons in situations outside the church community entirely, should be enabled to recognize more clearly the ministry of deacons as a unique vehicle for the Church's mission in the world. And deacons guided by the models, to the extent their circumstances allow, should become more effective diaconal ministers for the Church and in the world of today.

Second, the models are useful if they provide reliable criteria for a deacon's own discernment about concrete choices in ministry. Ideally, with the help of a spiritual director, the deacon could consider specific aspects of his situation and development as a minister in light of the goal of growing into full diaconal identity as an icon of Christ the servant and a minister of the

117

threshold. The situations examined may include the choices between and balance among ministry assignments; relations with other ministers and with the lay faithful; the balance of ministry with family, work, or other commitments; or the deacon's manner of representing Christ and the Church to others. The models give concreteness to a basic question in ministerial self-discernment: Am I moving toward the fullest diaconal identity possible for me under the circumstances?

Finally, these models should provide a reliable guide for the selection, formation, and assignment of deacons by vocation directors, formators, diaconate directors, bishops, pastors, and supervisors. The models do this by giving concreteness and definition to the goal of diaconal ministry, an important criterion for decision-making in these contexts. In the selection process, it can be asked whether inquirers or candidates, under the guidance of the Spirit and with the support of the Church, seem likely to grow into an icon of Christ the servant and minister of the threshold. Directors of formation may ask, Are we forming candidates for the full diaconal identity reflected by these models? Church leaders may ask how deacons in ministry should be assigned and supported so that they become the best possible icons of Christ the servant and ministers of the threshold.

THE TYPICAL CONTEXT OF DIACONAL MINISTRY

Though every deacon's life and ministry have individual characteristics, some broadly applicable factors in Church, society, and culture shape that personal situation. As already described in chapter 1, the vast majority of deacons exercise their ministry in a context, found in Western Europe and North America, that has become the typical one for the diaconate. This context has three characteristics that were surveyed in that chapter, and they can be reviewed briefly here. First, the diaconate has grown up during a rapid fall in the number of priests and a rise in ministry activities by the nonordained faithful, both volunteers and those employed by the Church. Second, the vast majority of deacons are married and earn a living in nonchurch jobs, and even if they are widowed or retired from such employment, this has been their defining profile for much of their lives. Most of a deacon's life, accordingly, is spent in conditions very much like the nonordained faithful, and indeed like the those who are outside the Church entirely. Finally, the outlook and culture of North America and Western Europe, the typical locus of diaconal ministry, is increasingly post-Christian and indeed nonreligious.

Chapter 11 will consider implications for the two models if the current situation changes, or if other typical contexts develop in the future. But in the contemporary world, this typical situation is strongly marked and provides us with well-defined contours against which we can test the practical usefulness of the two models.

CHRIST THE SERVANT

Chapter 7 explored the three dimensions—functional, relational, and sacramental—that make up the office of deacon. The image of Christ the servant has some broad practical implications in each of the three dimensions. We begin by defining those implications before moving on to apply them more specifically to the everyday context of diaconal ministry. On the functional side, the model reflects how Christ serves the this-worldly needs of those who suffer within a broader ministry incorporating proclamation and prayer. The model thus undergirds the foundational understanding of the diaconal tasks as integrating word, liturgy, and charity, with a center of gravity in charity. In the relational sphere, Christ the servant is the model for the deacon's liturgical ministry of assistance; for his position of service to the bishop, to the people of God, and to the Church's mission in the world; and for a ministry clearly distanced from power and status in the Church and in the world. The sacramentality of a deacon's ministry is the call to represent all the facets of Christ the servant in speech, action, and life. Specifically, Christ the servant is the guiding image for a distinct ministerial self-presentation: humble, but not servile; leading through service.

These practical implications of the model of Christ the servant give diaconal ministry distinctness and help to guide its practice in the typical context—ecclesial, social, and cultural—where that ministry is practiced. In a Church faced with a shrinking priesthood and a growth in various kinds of lay ministry, an insistence on integrating three tasks with a focus on charity makes deacons recognizably different from priests and bishops and also from lay ministers. Of course, the ideal balance between tasks is not always possible amid the various needs that dictate a deacon's ministerial assignments. Nevertheless, to exercise diaconal ministry authentically is to keep that ideal balance in view as a goal, and to move toward it as circumstances permit. Even in a situation where formal assignments are heavily tilted toward liturgical/sacramental roles, for example—where the deacon is being pressured to become a minipriest—it is worth exploring how this imbalance may be compensated for outside of formal assignments, in everyday life, through charitable encounters and attempts to share the gospel. The vocation to a full diaconal identity points to a similar need to rebalance or compensate when a deacon's assignments are strongly focused in other areas that may privilege one of the tasks, whether this may be administration, teaching, or charitable service. For bishops, diaconate directors, or pastors who give or approve these assignments, it is just as crucial to keep the functional balance of the tasks in view, in order both that the individual deacon may live his calling and that the diaconate may make its distinctive contribution to the Church's ministries.

In all of these decisions about ministry, moreover, the model of Christ the servant also reminds us how expansively the task of charity is to be understood. It is not just "How many hours am I devoting to the soup kitchen?"—as important as that service is. Modeled on the charity of Christ the servant, the deacon's charitable task is a call to participate in and represent in a particularly intense way Christ's special care for those who suffer in body, mind, or spirit, and particularly those who suffer unjustly. The model also shows *how* to carry out this task: nourished by, and where appropriate expressing explicitly, the gospel proclamation and the Church's life of prayer and liturgy.

The Models as Guides to Ministry in Practice

By framing the deacon's activity in liturgy and sacraments as an assisting one, the model of Christ the servant gives deacons a distinct liturgical role and offers a useful guide for the collaboration between deacons and priests or bishops in this sphere. The deacon's distinctiveness tends to become blurred in the eyes of the faithful when deacons take on more responsibilities for baptisms, weddings, funerals, and public worship like adoration, all of which in the diaconate's typical context were once normally performed by priests, who are becoming scarcer. However, the clearly assisting, nonpresiding role of the deacon in the Eucharist, and the fact that the other sacramental roles (as well as preaching at Mass) are delegated under pastoral oversight, help to keep the distinction in view.

The diaconate has also developed in a Church blessed by a significant increase in ministerial activities by people who are not ordained, many of whom exercise those ministries in a highly committed or even full-time manner. Of these, some—for example, pastoral associates, directors of faith formation, coordinators and directors of significant parish or diocesan programs—may have greater training or may be said to give greater service to the Church than deacons typically do. In this context, the model of Christ the servant strengthens diaconal ministry itself and provides guidance for a deacon's interactions with other ministers and parish or diocesan staff. The model frames the intrinsic functions of diaconal ministry through the three interrelated tasks, not in a deacon's particular assignments or job descriptions, and in this way distinguishes diaconal identity from the profile of ministers who undertake specific functions for a given time. Moreover, the mode of humble service and the distancing of diaconal office from status and power are expressed with particular clarity by the image of Christ the servant. This makes that model a useful reminder to the deacon to avoid "pulling rank" on nonordained ministers, particularly as they struggle to gain recognition in a Church where ministry has long been so identified with clerical power.

This model also provides important guidance for a deacon's collaboration with priests and bishops. Through its explicit appeal to Christ, the model offers a compelling image of servanthood that is not servile: in his obedient service to the Father, in his service to the spread of the kingdom, Jesus was no "respecter of persons." The model reminds us that the Church ordains deacons to service, not to become institutional order takers. The promise of obedience to the bishop places the objective conditions of diaconal ministry in a context of supervision, but it does not take away the deacon's own calling to live out both his baptismal promises and the full scope of his calling to the diaconate. While serving conscientiously within the context of local needs and organizational structures, then, deacons are also called to live out the dignity and fullness of the diaconal tasks, to avoid complicity in institutional sin, and to resist contributing to organizational dysfunction. To do so may require a deacon to stand up to those who have supervisory authority over him, or to resign an assignment. For the process of discerning how to live out this calling in practical situations, Christ the servant is a reliable guide.

In the area of diaconal leadership, about which unfortunately the diaconate literature continues to exhibit ambivalence, the model of Christ the servant has clear, practical, and indeed prophetic applications. In pointing to a mode of servant leadership exercised for the good of the people of God, the model shows how a deacon should lead within the local community: in a collaborative, noncompetitive way. Following *Lumen Gentium*, moreover, this kind of servant leadership, modeled on Christ the servant, is the basis of all leadership by bishops and priests as well: the deacon is tasked with representing this way of leading in a particularly clear way for the whole Church, and in this way helping to undermine tendencies to clericalism and institutional turf building.[1]

The model of Christ the servant provides deacons with a particularly effective ministerial identity in the social, familial, and workplace conditions of life that deacons share with the laity and with those outside the church community. Deacons have the capacity to bring a distinct ecclesial presence to those situations owing to their permanent, public, and sacramental commitment to the Church's mission. Depending on the particular context, this presence may be more or less clearly understood by those around them, but at the least it is always implicit. As an ordained minister with a specifically serving role that is distanced from Church power, the deacon can seem approachable to some who would not seek out a priest or bishop precisely because of their greater authority. (Of course, there are people who may never have occasion to meet a priest or bishop, either.) This quality of approachability gives the deacon opportunities to extend an invitation from the Church and eventually to the Church. Approachability is by no means exclusive to deacons, of course: there are people who say, "I want to see a priest," just as there are others who will be drawn to someone in a religious order or to a faithful layperson. Yet deacons have a distinct profile, and in everyday situations people approach them for prayers and blessings, for sick visits, for counsel, as a listening ear, or to stand up against an injustice. These requests and opportunities come not primarily because of the deacon's personal qualities, but because he is representing the Church's diaconate as an icon of Christ the servant.

In a culture that is increasingly post-Christian and nonreligious, the deacon's ecclesial presence without the trappings of power, an identity rooted in the model of Christ the servant, provides a unique kind of opening for dialogue and eventual evangelization. This culture has a suspicion of authority and often treats truth claims, including religious ones, as expressions of power and domination: that assumption underpins many popular criticisms of, and resentments against, faith and the Church. A deacon who identifies with Christ the humble servant, who shares with others an ordinary social life, has fewer roadblocks to conversation about faith in this cultural milieu than priests or bishops do, while at the same time expressing an ecclesial identity that adds a particular rootedness to Christian discipleship in general. Moreover, the unifying emphasis within diaconal ministry on humble and charitable service provides a particularly effective way of bringing a recognizable ecclesial presence into everyday life, since in this culture word and sacrament are becoming harder for many people to comprehend.

At the same time, the deacon as icon of Christ the servant is a profoundly countercultural figure in a world where truth is often seen as relative and commitments as provisional. Deacons represent, both within and beyond the Church, an unflinching, lifelong commitment to serve the truth of the gospel and the Church's mission. This commitment to serve, when the deacon represents it clearly and thus sacramentally, may attract attitudes of fascination, respect, envy, puzzlement, incomprehension, suspicion, or resentment. Here the minister modeled on Christ the servant has been brought to that place of tension, the threshold between Church and world, human and divine realities, that is most strongly expressed in our second model.

MINISTER OF THE THRESHOLD

This model, too, offers a guide to practical ministry for the diaconate in each of its three dimensions. In the sphere of function, a ministry of the threshold is a mission to the margins of the church community, both to those unable to join the eucharistic assembly (the homebound, patients in hospitals, residents in nursing or assisted living facilities, prisoners) and to those who simply are not coming (the indifferent, the ambivalent, the unconnected, the resentful, the estranged). Within the church community itself this mission goes out especially to those who are overlooked or not fully accepted; to those who feel marginalized, or whose sufferings or doubts cut them off from full participation. As a minister of the threshold the deacon is primarily related not, as in the model of Christ the servant, to the bishop and to God's people, but rather to the threshold dimension of the Church: to the threshold between sanctuary and worshipers, the Church and the world, divine and human realities. Especially in relation to the Church and the world, the ministry of the threshold has a two-way movement: out from the Church as the bearer of the gospel, back to the Church with an invitation to the eucharistic banquet and to life in God. In its sacramentality, the ministry of the threshold also represents a key aspect of the Church: not primarily the Church already gathered, but a dynamic Church with a mission to its frontiers, outward-turning, inviting, and gathering in.

124

In the ecclesial situation in which the diaconate has grown, as the priesthood has decreased in numbers while nonordained ministries have grown, the threshold model points to distinctive characteristics of the diaconate that complement those expressed by the model of Christ the servant. A diaconal ministry oriented to the threshold is clearly recognizable as different from the ministry of priests and bishops, whose primary, though not sole, orientation is toward the gathered community, expressed in eucharistic presiding and pastoral oversight. Nor is the deacon's ministry of the threshold, with all the facets surveyed in chapter 9, quite the equivalent of any nonordained ministry, even one dedicated to evangelization or outreach or service to the homebound. These ministries are not rooted to the same extent in liturgy and they do not have the same permanent and public commitment that comes from ordination. Only the diaconate is modeled on a ministry of the threshold in all its dimensions.

This distinctive profile and purpose that the threshold model gives to diaconal ministry also provides useful criteria for concrete decisions about how to practice it. Certainly, this model, without denying the rooting of all diaconal ministry in prayer and liturgy, points deacons away from an excessive tilt toward sacramental roles, liturgical preaching, and involvement in ongoing parish programs, as important as all these are. Particularly in the current climate with its pressures to fill in for a shrinking priesthood, the deacon who becomes too strongly identified with these roles is no longer a deacon but a minipriest. To overcome such a pull does not mean that every deacon must have a significant formal assignment in a food pantry, homeless shelter, prison, or nursing home. Nor is a ministry of the threshold detached from word and liturgy: a diaconal mission to the margins, including home or hospital visits or calls to parishioners in need, always includes implicitly, and often explicitly, sharing God's word, the Eucharist, or prayers and blessings.

A ministry of the threshold has an important dimension within the gathered community (such as the parish), and in practicing it the deacon need not distance himself from the community's most active and contributing members. But a minister of the threshold consciously seeks out those within the community who are overlooked, struggling to find a place, or isolated by suffering. An authentic ministry of the threshold moves back and forth between the Church's central liturgical gathering and those at the community's margins. For the deacon ministering in the gathered community, then, the threshold model suggests two practical questions: Am I overly identified with the priest/presider, with the leadership, with the community's "in-crowd"?[2] Are my heart and mind and action strongly given over to the needs of those who are counted least, who are forgotten, who live at the community's margins?

An authentic ministry of the threshold conditions a deacon's participation in the liturgy itself, and in this the model takes us beyond the indications found in the image of Christ the servant, which mainly underpins the deacon's assisting/serving role. We already noted in the last chapter how in the Mass the deacon moves across the sanctuary threshold in speech and action, and how this movement adds dynamism to the interplay between the celebrant and the worshipers. There are several concrete ways, beyond the minimum liturgical requirement of conscious and reverent participation, in which deacons can make this dynamic interplay clearer and more alive. One is by bringing the threshold perspective to preaching, both in the sense of representing the needs and aspirations of those at the margins of the community, and in channeling into the homily the experience of living at the threshold between Church and world. Another is by consciously gathering up the penitential and intercessory prayers for the people, rather than simply reciting them. The final dismissal, in which the deacon sends forth the community to participate in their common mission across the threshold, is a particularly visible liturgical expression of this model of diaconal ministry. These threshold dimensions of a deacon's liturgical role become clearer when consciously expressed, and even more so if the deacon's everyday practice of ministry is recognized by the community as guided by the threshold model.

Deacons spend most of their lives in the social conditions they share with the lay faithful and with those outside the Church. They do not check their permanent, sacramentally formed identity as an ecclesial minister at the church door; this identity is present and has the potential for expression at any hour of any day. Yet deacons have a secular identity, too, formed through family, work, civic and social activities, and personal interests. Deacons live on the threshold between these two identities, and each deacon navigates the threshold differently. In some everyday situations, the ecclesial identity can be expressed very openly; in others that identity remains largely implicit. In navigating this threshold, a deacon needs to be attentive to his effect on others, and to value the feedback and criticisms of those who know him best. When lived authentically, this threshold is a place of inner tension, of possibility, of creative growth. In reflecting on his life in the world in light of the threshold model, then, the deacon might ask questions like the following: Is my life in the world transformed and redirected by my ecclesial identity? Have I made that identity recognizable in a way that is both inviting and challenging to those around me? Have I discerned the possibilities and constraints of my situation in the world for a minister of the Church, and acted accordingly?

A minister of the threshold represents the Church in its outer-directed movement, and this indicates that true diaconal ministry should have a center of gravity outside the Church. To see what this means in practice, imagine the ministry of a deacon focused primarily inside the Church: liturgical roles, parish programs, pastoral service in the community. Then imagine this deacon living a good and perhaps even holy life in the world, but a life in which his identity as a minister of the Church is largely implicit. The threshold model suggests two ways that this ministry can become more authentically diaconal. At the level of formal ministry assignments, is it possible to move outward toward the margins of the church community (through some home or hospital visits, for example, or in some other way) or outside it, among those in the wider society who are poor and suffering? And in everyday life, can the deacon make an ecclesial presence somehow more explicit and more inviting?

By living authentically at the threshold place between the Church and the world, deacons are a particularly apt vehicle of grace and witness in a secular, post-Christian culture. Christianity views the human person as having a source and final destiny in God, while truly living a this-worldly existence. Every human being, then, lives at the threshold between an ordinary life conditioned by sin and death, and the dynamic call and indwelling of the Spirit. Our secular culture tends to deny or minimize the spiritual; and yet contemporary people bound by such a limited worldview still have a restlessness, a yearning, that points beyond their self-imposed limits. The deacon's threshold place between Church and world, between ecclesial and secular identities, can provide a particularly concrete image of the full humanity to which Christian faith witnesses. By living within and out of this threshold place, the deacon's presence in the everyday world is a riddle for secular culture, which can be challenged to ask, Is there something more?

THE PERSONAL CONTEXT AND THE LIMITS OF THE MODELS

The models of Christ the servant and minister of the threshold are designed to provide a guide specifically for the ministerial identity of deacons. While that identity touches every part of a deacon's life, it is not the deacon's whole person. All questions about ministerial goals and activities arise within a personal situation incorporating other dimensions.

Some aspects of a deacon's personal context may be mentioned briefly here. Choices and assignments in ministry must be consonant with a deacon's physical and mental health, gifts, and shortcomings. They also must be consistent with his basic calling, sealed by baptism and confirmation, as a Christian disciple: with the life of prayer and with Christian ethical standards in his treatment of self and others. In particular, though any authentic ministry involves some suffering and sacrifice, no ministry should be physically or emotionally depleting, spiritually deadening, or unethical in its goals and practice. Further, the commitment to ministry coexists with other commitments in every deacon's life. Crucially, most deacons also have a commitment to marriage that is prior to the diaconate: prior in time, prior as a claim, and prior sacramentally. Many deacons also have family responsibilities, often with obligations to provide care. And deacons typically are responsible, in whatever way their circumstances require, for earning a living.

Personal circumstances like these may suggest possibilities for diaconal ministry, or they may impose constraints on it. Our two models, accordingly, must be placed in a larger context. In a general way, we can express this placement as follows: the deacon's ministerial identity, when guided by the models of Christ the servant and minister of the threshold, must also be integrated within a fully rounded human life of Christian discipleship.

CHAPTER ELEVEN

• • • • • •

CONCLUSION AND A GLANCE AT THE FUTURE

This book began in chapter 1 with a question: Who are deacons and what are they tasked to do? The next nine chapters provide the answer: the Church is calling them to be icons of Christ the servant and ministers of the threshold. These two models are rooted in the person and activity of Christ and in the mission of the Church. They incorporate characteristics of a deacon's everyday ministerial experience: the assisting role in liturgy, the three tasks integrated in a single ministry with a focus on charity, the experience of ministering from an in-between place in the Church and in the world. As fully developed, complementary models, they give concrete definition to a deacon's functions, express both the distinct profile of diaconal office and its set of relationships within the Church and the world, and define a style of ministerial self-presentation and action. These models, in short, express who deacons are and show what they are tasked to do. They provide a theologically cogent and practically useful vision of the ministerial identity of deacons in the Church.

A BACKWARD LOOK: THE GENESIS, DEVELOPMENT, AND DEFINING CHARACTERISTICS OF THE MODELS

The models draw inspiration and fundamental patterns from some of the earliest texts of the Christian faith. The commissioning of the Seven in Acts 6:1–6, though not an account of the first ordination of deacons, provides a pattern for the integration of word, liturgy, and charity into a single ministry patterned on that of Christ and the first apostles. 1 Timothy 3:1–13, an exhortation in time of crisis to deacons and to the community overseers who later would be called bishops, already assumes a stable diaconal office with multiple functions assisting the local leadership in a relation of close collaboration. The letter calls on deacons to be examples of the Christian life for the community. Ignatius and Polycarp extend and deepen this exemplifying role by exhorting deacons to model Christ the servant in an image that would be picked up and developed by the Second Vatican Council.

In the West, the diaconate of the early Church developed, by the Middle Ages, into merely a stepping-stone to the priesthood, which came to constitute the defining office of ordained ministry. Fast-forward a thousand years to the mid-twentieth century: a movement springs up seeking to address contemporary pastoral and mission needs by restoring the diaconate as a permanent ministry. From the beginning, proponents see this diaconal ministry as having an orientation to service, especially to the needy, and thus a calling distinct from the priesthood. They also imagine deacons, living with their families in non-church surroundings, as ministers with a bridge or mediating role between the Eucharist and ordinary life, or with a distinct focus to the margins of the gathered church. These leading ideas, rooted as they are both in the pastoral challenges of the day and in theological reflection about ordained ministry, provide a solid foundation for the two complementary models of diaconal identity, Christ the servant and minister of the threshold, that developed after the council.

Vatican II (1962–65) provided a forum for deciding whether to allow the diaconate to become a permanent ministry again. The final decision, with optional implementation by regional bishop's conferences and the continuing requirement of celibacy for candidates not yet of "mature age," offers a notably cautious pastoral solution. This helps to explain the uneven growth of the diaconate in the ensuing years, against ongoing skepticism and pockets of opposition. Since 1968, when Pope St. Paul VI authorized bishops' conferences to request implementation of the diaconate, a heavy majority of the world's deacons, now numbering over 46,000, have been ordained in North America and parts of Western Europe.[1] This means that diaconal ministry largely has been shaped and reflected upon in this context of a shrinking priesthood and an increasingly post-Christian culture.

A careful reading of the key council texts presents deacons as "serving" ministers, whose identity is sketched briefly, with the help of a quote from Polycarp, in the image of Christ the servant, thus giving a conciliar grounding for this model of the diaconate, which became dominant after the council. During this time, the appeals to Christ the servant have offered few specifics about the image or its implications, but the model has still attracted criticism. Meanwhile, theologians have continued to explore the diaconate as a bridge or mediating ministry that is exercised characteristically at the margins or threshold of the Church. Those explorations, while often theologically suggestive and capable of pointing to distinctive ministerial initiatives for deacons, have seldom been in conversation with each other and generally lack any broader theological framework that might connect them. In a general way, then, ideas about the diaconate as a ministry specially devoted to Christian service, oriented somehow to the margins or the threshold, have become incorporated into the self-understanding of deacons, and into decisions about formation and assignments, in the years since the council. The models of Christ the servant and minister of the threshold, in fact, are drawn from formulations whose widespread use, whether implicit or explicit, has already shown them to be intelligible, inspiring, and practical. The goal of this book has been to structure, clarify, and deepen these already-existing formulations.

Conclusion and a Glance at the Future

The model of Christ the servant, once carefully defined, highlights the diaconate's assisting role in liturgy, its focus on this-worldly charity within a full ministry incorporating word and sacrament, and the emphasis on service rather than power in its style of ministry and leadership. The model also provides a foundation for the importance, in the deacon's pattern of relationships, on service: to the bishop, to the people of God, and to the Church's mission in the world. In a broadly sacramental way, deacons are called to be icons of Christ the servant through a ministerial self-presentation that is humble without being servile and expresses a public and permanent commitment to serve the furthering of God's kingdom of charity and justice.

The threshold model presented in this book connects earlier suggestions—that deacons have a bridge or mediating role within the gathered church, and also a distinct ministry to the margins—into a single image rooted in the threshold dimension of Christ's person and activity. This model complements that of Christ the servant, in part, by reflecting the widespread experience of deacons as ministering from an "in-between" place in the Church and world. The threshold image highlights the deacon's liturgical role moving between sanctuary and worshipers, in action and speech, during the Eucharist; the particular orientation to those at the margins of the Church and in the broader society; and the special springboard for witness to the gospel given to an ordained minister who shares the social life of the lay faithful and of the wider world. In a broadly sacramental way deacons are called to model Christ and his Body, the Church, in their movement across social and institutional thresholds, sharing the good news and inviting all into a fuller life with God.

These models, applied to diaconal ministry in its typical Western context, render that ministry more practically effective and also more recognizably distinct among the Church's ministries. The models also provide useful goals and criteria for self-discernment by deacons and for decisions about vocations, formation, and assignments by those responsible for diaconal ministry in the Church. The particular applications, covered in chapter 10, show the models to be practically useful as well as theologically coherent. To be concrete and useful, of course, these models must reflect a real-life context in the Church and in the world. With a glance to the future, we must ask how the models would address changes in that context. But first we turn to a situation in the Church today that presents a challenge to the development of an authentic ministerial identity for deacons everywhere.

A CONTEMPORARY CHALLENGE: TWO DIACONATES?

We noted in chapter 3 that by the 1950s, the transitional diaconate leading to priesthood, although the Western Church's sole norm for over a thousand years, was an anomaly in certain respects, particularly as a sacramentally ordained ministry without any independent ministerial rationale. This diaconate is still the universal norm in the Catholic Church, where it now exists alongside a "permanent" diaconate.[2] The revival of a diaconal office with its own ministerial purpose and identity has resulted in a theological and ministerial tension between these two diaconates, most visible in those places where the lifelong diaconate has grown to include large numbers.

It is not our purpose here to enter into the question of whether the practice of ordination through grades, specifically from diaconate to priesthood, is good theology for priestly ministry and for the sacrament of holy orders. Strictly from the standpoint of the ministerial identity of deacons, however, the ongoing presence of a parallel diaconate leading to priesthood causes confusion and poses a challenge. The two diaconates have the same ordination rite, but for two different purposes. What does this say about the meaning of the ordination itself? In general, the transitional diaconate period is used as training for priesthood, giving these deacons exactly the profile of mini-priests that undermines the development of a full diaconal identity for deacons who make a lifelong commitment. The training model for transitional deacons also particularly stresses the functional aspects of the diaconate, and even these functions are often limited in the training to liturgical and pastoral tasks. To the extent this profile leaks into the understanding of a lifelong

134

diaconal ministry, the relational and sacramental dimensions of diaconal ministry are compromised. The transitional diaconate, then, presents a constant challenge for the actualization of a full diaconal identity modeled on Christ the servant and a ministry of the threshold.

There are two possible ways of overcoming this challenge permanently. The first would be to abolish the transitional diaconate, as Paul VI did with the subdiaconate and the minor orders in 1972.[3] The second would be for transitional deacons to be formed, through both teaching and supervision, with the authentic ministerial identity of the diaconate (adapted to their situation as celibate seminarians) before ordination to the priesthood: focused on the integrity of the three tasks with a center of gravity in charity, inspired by the model of Christ the servant, and practicing a ministry to the margins of the gathered church. In defense of this second option, it can be argued that the diaconal form of service is the foundation of all ordained ministry, and that priesthood and then episcopacy build upon this foundation to form that ministry in its fullness. From a practical viewpoint, too, if priests were formed first as deacons, they would likely be more effective in collaborating with and supervising deacons later. To question whether either of these options is prudent or theologically defensible would take us beyond the scope of this book. In any case, there seems no prospect of either option becoming a reality within the foreseeable future.

The practical challenge to diaconal identity posed by the current situation may be mitigated to the extent and in the places that the Church ordains many deacons to lifelong ministry, and their ministerial presence in the Church overshadows the brief passage of transitional deacons in local communities. In addition, both Church leaders and the people in the pews may come to accept as settled that there are two offices with the same name, but with different purposes, each of which must be understood on its own terms.

Taking the situation as a given, the models of Christ the servant and minister of the threshold address the resulting challenge directly. They provide support and clarity to diaconal identity by framing the diaconate not with reference to priesthood, which is the defining aim for transitional deacons, but by rooting diaconal ministry directly and independently in the person and activity of Christ, and in the Church's mission.

A GLANCE AT THE FUTURE: HOW THE MODELS COULD ADDRESS CHANGES IN CHURCH MINISTRIES

We noted in chapter 10 that the two models are not designed primarily to describe a ministerial situation as it is; instead, they hold out a goal. Yet they would not be intelligible or useful if they did not reflect some basic characteristics of the ministry as it is actually practiced. The models have been developed in the context of Western Europe and North America over the past fifty years. The vast majority of deacons, though certainly not each and every one, exhibit characteristics from this context, which therefore can be called typical, as noted already in chapter 1. The specific characteristics that have had the most influence in framing the two models involve the contrasting situations of deacons and priests. In the typical Western context we find increasing numbers of deacons who typically are married, earn a living in nonchurch jobs, and serve local Catholic communities in a functionally volunteer capacity.[4] And we find decreasing numbers of priests whose ministry is strongly marked by the presiding role at the Eucharist and often by pastoring roles as well, doing ministry as a profession and living unmarried in rectories or religious houses. The contrast between these two situations exerts an influence, though not a defining one, on the way the models express the distinct identity of deacons, particularly their serving role and their "in-between" social location. If and when these characteristics change and the diaconate grows in different contexts, the models could reflect less clearly the situation deacons face in their everyday ministry. A few possible changes, their likely implications, and ways in which the models could address them, may be suggested here.

First, if the scarcity of priests reaches a point where the typical responsibility for deacons involves gathering and administering local communities, deacons come to act as pastors and look increasingly like priests with limitations. The servant aspects of a deacon's identity, and the particular orientation to the threshold dimension of the Church and the world, become less clear than when deacons and priests have their distinct roles side by side.

The danger of deacons devolving into local minipastors may be less if the priest scarcity is of long standing, as foreseen in Vatican II's Decree on Missionary Activity *Ad Gentes*, where deacons are pictured as "leading far-flung communities in the name of the bishop or parish priest."[5] The confusion of roles also could be less if the deacon's oversight responsibilities were understood as temporary or atypical, required for example by social upheavals, political persecution, or relatively short-term adjustments in the structure of ministry. In both these situations, the deacon's "servant" role toward the bishop, the Church, and the local community may remain relatively clear; and the community to which he is sent to minister has itself become the threshold of the Church, so the deacon remains a minister of the threshold. However, to the extent the deacon-run parish should become a typical case, the hold of the threshold and servant models of diaconal identity would be weakened, and the diaconate as a distinct ministry in the Church would be impoverished.[6] Even here, however, the models could suggest ways the deacon could compensate for the anomalous ministry situation so as to keep a distinctly diaconal identity alive.

Second, to the extent the social profile of priests becomes more like that lived by deacons in the current typical situation for the diaconate, the distinctive "in-between" locus of diaconal ministry that contributes to the threshold model becomes less recognizable. There are several ways this could happen, and the potential blurring of roles is a matter of degree. If priests in large numbers were to marry and have families, this would take away one difference, although one could question whether the distinct profile of deacons among the Eastern Rite Catholics and Orthodox Christians has been compromised by a married priesthood. A more important movement toward blending roles would arise if priests typically earned their livelihood outside the ministry, in secular occupations, a possible development in some (non-Western) contexts where the economic burden of a professional priesthood may be too great. Yet even if deacons and priests lived in largely similar conditions, the deacon's distinct servant identity, along with a ministry of the threshold (liturgically, in the community, and in the world) could be maintained. These changes in the social and economic context of priesthood, then, seem less of a threat to diaconal identity than the practice of deacons typically taking on the oversight role of pastors.

Finally, changes in the profile of the diaconate itself could affect the descriptive grounding of the two models. Three changes with potential effects may be considered. First, would the diaconal identity defined here need to be altered if the Church should allow women to be ordained to the diaconate? The answer is no: both the servant and threshold dimensions of this ministerial identity do not in principle specify male or female. The theological rationales put forth in support of the current discipline include the arguments that based on Scripture and Tradition the Church does not have the authority to ordain a woman; or that the unity of Holy Orders requires that only a man may be ordained; or that a woman because of her gender is not able to be the icon of Christ.[7] If any of these arguments is accepted, the theological conclusion is that only a man can be ordained a deacon, and therefore only a man can have the ministerial identity defined in this book. On the other hand, proponents of changing the current discipline to allow the ordination of women to the diaconate argue that the early Church ordained women to the diaconate on the same basis as men, that there is no reason the Church may not revive this practice, and that women are as able as men to exercise diaconal ministry, including its sacramental representation of Christ.[8] If these arguments are accepted, the theological conclusion is that the Church may ordain women to the diaconate, and therefore women deacons could have the ministerial identity defined in this book. In either case, it is not a ministerial identity based on Christ the servant and minister of the threshold that tips the scales. This debate is about who should be ordained a deacon, and not about the ministerial identity of a deacon once ordained—the subject of this book.

Second, if more members of religious orders are ordained to the diaconate (currently this is a very small number),[9] the usual "nonchurch" social location of deacons that contributes to the threshold model would be absent. However, to the extent the charism of the religious order allows, a ministerial orientation toward the threshold remains possible, even in a cloistered community, for example in the care of the sick or of visitors. Another possibility: if more deacons become Church professionals, particularly in parish or diocesan staff positions, the workplace location ceases to be a place of threshold ministry in the same way it is for deacons who work in secular jobs.[10] Yet deacons can compensate for this by committing to such a ministry outside the workplace, either in formal assignments or informal interactions.

These situations, while hardly exhausting the possible conditions in which deacons could be challenged to live an authentic ministry, do illustrate different contexts than the Western one over the past fifty years, in which the models of Christ the servant and minister of the threshold have been developed. In general, the models would still apply usefully to these different situations, or point to ways of complementing ministries that are not fully diaconal. The survey of possible changes suggests the resilience of the two models when applied to different contexts. At the same time, it is worth repeating that the Western context within which the practical implications of the models were tested in chapter 10 looks to be the typical one for the foreseeable future.

THE FLEXIBILITY, RESILIENCE, AND INNER UNITY OF THE MODELS

If the models prove to be as applicable to different contexts as this brief survey has suggested, the reason lies in the way they are designed. While the models have a descriptive grounding in ministerial practice, they are rooted more fundamentally in the mysteries of Christ and the Church, and they point to goals rather than describing practice. The goals are concrete and specific to diaconal ministry, but they are not so detailed as to apply only to particular conditions. Indeed, the key metaphors, servant and threshold, are many-sided and open to further reflection, both theological and practical. One can always ask, Are there other ways a deacon may be an icon of Christ the servant? Are there new thresholds a deacon may be called to cross?

Most of this book has been concerned with defining the two models in parallel, giving each one as much theological weight and practical usefulness as possible on its own. We have also noted that the two models complement each other. They highlight different but, in each case, fundamental characteristics of a deacon's ministry. Overall, the metaphor of Christ the servant offers a more static vision of where the deacon is placed within the Church and its ministries, while the image of a minister of the threshold emphasizes dynamism and movement, both within and beyond the gathered Church. The model of Christ the servant begins by stopping the deacon long enough to take stock of where he is; the threshold model starts by pointing the direction the deacon must go. Diaconal ministry becomes complete, distinctive, and authentic only when guided by both models together.

The two models, moreover, reinforce each other and, at a deep level, combine into a single, rounded vision of the deacon's ministerial identity. They spring, after all, from reflection on the one person of Christ. As servant of the Father, Christ the humble servant who stretched out his arms on the cross for our salvation is the same Christ who, precisely to effect that salvation, passed through social thresholds and invited the world to cross the threshold into God's kingdom. There is no threshold mission in Christ that is not an expression of servanthood, and no servanthood in Christ that does not stretch over the threshold to invite us to share in God's life.

The deacon, too, when guided by the image of Christ the servant, necessarily stretches across thresholds to those at the margins, both within the gathered community and in the wider world, with the invitation to fullness of life in Christ. The two models, then, point toward a single identity in ministry: the one to which the Church calls deacons. And this ministry is the gift that deacons offer to the Church.

• • • • • •

ACTS 6:1–6

Springboard of the Gentile Mission

In chapter 2 we saw that the commissioning of the Seven in Acts 6:1–6 provides a model or "type" for diaconal ministry, rather than an account of the first ordination of deacons. That reading of the passage as a foundation story, however, has such weight in tradition that it may be called the traditional view. To reject this interpretation decisively it is necessary to show that the commissioning story has a well-defined but different function in the narrative of Acts. The incident does have such a function. The commissioning serves as the jumping-off point for a much larger theme: the widening mission to the Gentiles, which will culminate in the Apostle Paul's residence in Rome itself, the center of the Gentile world (28:14–31). This appendix provides the exegetical support for reading Acts 6:1–6 as a springboard for that Gentile mission. We begin with the following literal translation. The Greek words that have connected the passage to the diaconate are in parentheses.

> [6:1] In those days, as the disciples were increasing in number, grumbling arose against the Hebrews among the Hellenists, because their widows were being over-looked in the daily ministry (*diakonia*). [2] The Twelve summoned the community of the disciples and said, "It is not right that we should neglect the Word of

God to do ministry at tables (*diakonein trapezais*). [3] So look about among you, brothers, for seven men of good reputation who are full of the Spirit and of wisdom whom we may appoint to that task; [4] whereas we will continue to devote ourselves to prayer and the ministry (*diakonian*) of the Word." [5] What the Twelve said found favor with the whole community. They chose Stephen, a man full of faith and of the Holy Spirit, together with Philip, Prochorus, Nicanor, Timon, Parmenas, and Nicolaus, who was a proselyte of Antioch. [6] These they set before the apostles, who prayed and laid hands upon them.

THE TRADITIONAL VIEW IN SCHOLARSHIP AND PREACHING

Contemporary Scripture scholars tend to choose one of three approaches to the traditional reading of this text as a foundation story for the office of deacon. Some just ignore the tradition and say nothing about any potential connection between this passage and the diaconate, focusing rather on whatever their exegesis of the passage uncovers—which obviously, for these scholars, is not the foundation of diaconal office.[1] Other commentators mention the traditional view as a possible interpretation and then pass on without evaluating it.[2] Still others accept that view as settled without examining whether a careful exegesis of the text in Acts actually supports it.[3] For their part, homilists on this passage may apply it directly to today's diaconate, either unaware of the exegetical difficulties or assuming that those problems have no bearing on the homiletic task. Among those who want to incorporate exegesis into their engagement with this text, however, there is unease about what it has to tell us about diaconal office, if it is not a foundation story. Chapter 2 addresses that unease by providing a typological reading that is strongly supported by the text and has specific implications for diaconal ministry.

PROBLEMS WITH THE TRADITIONAL VIEW

In the translation above, the inclusion in parentheses of the *diakon-* words that relate verbally to "deacon" suggest how the incident was connected to the diaconate. These *diakon-* words refer to ministry, agency (i.e., acting on behalf of someone else), or assistance in general, as well as to the diaconate as an office in particular. The shifting meanings in this word group are shown in the three contexts where they are used in the passage, and this sheds light on an uncertainty about what exactly the Seven are being commissioned to do. It is some kind of *diakonia*; the word *diakonos*, "deacon," itself is never used of the Seven or anyone else. The *diakonia* in 6:1 is often translated as food distribution, but the word simply means ministry or service in a general sense, as the literal, open-ended, and somewhat awkward translation here ("daily ministry") attempts to reflect. The context shows that the *diakonia* involves meeting some unmet needs of the widows, and 6:2 indicates that this *diakonia* is done at tables, so that the ministry for which the Seven are being commissioned is sometimes translated as "serving at table" or something similar, implying that the Seven are expected to serve or distribute food. But it is at least as likely, given the grammatical construction, that the tables are for distributing money, which would come out of the common fund described shortly before, at 4:34–35.[4] The text, then, does not present the Seven with any clarity as tables waiters. But the particular *diakonia* for which the Twelve commission them does seem to involve meeting physical needs.[5]

How did the Seven come to be understood as deacons? The earliest surviving document connecting the Seven with the diaconate is St. Irenaeus of Lyons's *Against All Heresies*, a work of doctrinal argument not directly concerned with questions of ministry or Church order from the third quarter of the second century. This work alludes in passing on three occasions to one or more of the Seven as deacons, treating the identification as something already commonly understood.[6] Irenaeus does not do any analysis of Acts 6:1-6 to suggest how this understanding developed, and the fact that the Seven are never called deacons (*diakonoi*) in the passage requires us to make our own guesses about how the connection had been made. One obvious link is word association. The task of the Seven is called *diakonia*, and the actual doing of this service is described by the verb *diakonein* (6:2). Beyond this word association, however, there must have been something about the deacons actually known to Irenaeus and his readers that connected them to ministry to the needy, and thereby to the Seven. And in fact, it does seem likely that early deacons had, among their responsibilities, that of distributing food and probably financial assistance, both to participants in community gatherings and to those not in attendance.[7]

Many writers after Irenaeus allude to this common understanding of the Seven as the first deacons, and the connection must have been strengthened by the apostles' laying hands upon them (6:6), an action that became characteristic of later ordination rites. Nevertheless, John Chrysostom, undertaking toward the end of the fourth century a more careful exegesis of the text itself in his *Homilies on Acts*, concludes that the Seven were commissioned solely for the limited task of taking care of the Hellenist widows in Jerusalem, and not for any wider ministry.[8] This negative view of the connection between deacons and the Seven remained the minority opinion until twentieth-century scholars undertook a more critical exploration of this passage and its place in the larger narrative arc of Acts.

There are many weaknesses in the traditional connection between the Seven and the office of deacon. The text never calls them deacons. Acts as a whole never mentions deacons. The words describing the ministries the Seven are tasked with (*diakonia, diakonein*) are too wide-ranging in their meaning (including ministry, service, acting as agent of another person) to suggest by word association a specific reference to *diakonos* as a Church office. Indeed, the term *diakonia* is applied equally to the ministry of the Word (6:4) the Twelve reserve to themselves.[9] Nor are the Seven ever shown fulfilling the supposedly diaconal tasks for which they have been chosen. Indeed, they are never mentioned again as a group—hardly the picture of a stable Church office.

THE LAUNCH OF THE GENTILE MISSION

Rather than exercising any stable office in the community, in fact, two of the Seven embark immediately on missions having nothing to do with the Hellenist widows but instead modeled on the ministries of the Twelve. Stephen performs signs and wonders (6:8), which must include healings, and preaches (7:2-53) with magnificent effect, exercising his gift of prophecy (6:10). Philip leaves Judea for Samaria, where he evangelizes (8:5), casts out demons and heals the sick (8:7), and apparently baptizes (8:12). Setting out later to Gaza, he teaches Scripture to the Ethiopian eunuch (8:26-35), baptizes him (8:36-38), and continues up the coast, evangelizing as he goes (8:40). In effect, the only two of the Seven we hear about become apostles, their specific actions modeled on and extending earlier acts by the Twelve.

Acts 6:1-6 provides a direct narrative connection between the Twelve and the ministry of Stephen and Philip through their inclusion in the commissioning of the Seven. But there is an inconsistency between what the Seven are commissioned to do and the functions Stephen and Philip actually take on. Yet, the commissioning event makes sense through its function in the narrative arc of Acts. The activities of Stephen and Philip extend the mission of the Twelve because Stephen's preaching causes a showdown with the temple leaders in Jerusalem (6:9-15; 7:54–8:3). This upheaval pushes the apostles' evangelization beyond the Jews to the Samaritans (8:4-17), the first step in the broader Gentile mission that is the central concern of Acts. The commissioning of the Seven, then, is readily explained as an event that furthers the narrative. But it does not suggest the establishment of a stable office with distinct functions of any kind, in particular not the office of the deacon as we will find it elsewhere, such as in 1 Timothy 3:8-13 or in the writings of Ignatius and Polycarp. Rather, the commissioning event is a key step in the broadening of the apostles' mission from Jerusalem to the known world.

• • • • • •

1 TIMOTHY 3:1–13

Exegesis and the Diaconal Functions

Drawing on 1 Timothy 3:1–13, chapter 2 found deacons to be holders of a stable office with multiple functions, exercised in a close relation of assistance to the overseer and tasked with modeling a life of Christian faith for the local community. This appendix reviews some of the exegesis underlying those conclusions and specifically digs more deeply into the text to show how it supports the view that diaconal office has multiple functions, rather than a single outstanding function, as is the case with a charism or spiritual gift.[1]

We begin with a literal translation:

[3:1] The saying is sure: If anyone aspires to the office of overseer (*episkopos*), he seeks out a noble task. [2] For an overseer (*episkopos*) must be above reproach, the husband of only one wife, sober, self-controlled, respectable, hospitable, skilled at teaching; [3] no drunkard; not violent, but rather forbearing; not quarrelsome or greedy. [4] He must supervise his own household well, keeping his children in line and his family notable for their seriousness; [5] for if a man does not know how to supervise his own household, how is he to look after God's church? [6] He is not to be a recent convert, lest he become puffed up and fall into the condemnation

146

reserved for the devil. [7] And he must have a good reputation among outsiders, lest he fall into disgrace and the snares of the devil.

[8] Deacons (*diakonoi*) likewise must be serious, not insincere, not addicted to much wine, not greedy for gain; [9] they must hold to the mystery of faith with a clean conscience. [10] Moreover they should be tested first, and only exercise ministry (*diakoneitōsan*) if they prove themselves blameless. [11] Women likewise must be serious, not slanderers, self-controlled, faithful in everything. [12] Deacons (*diakonoi*) must be husbands of only one wife and must supervise their own households and children well. [13] For those who minister (*diakonēsontes*) well earn a noble standing for themselves, and great confidence in the faith in Christ Jesus.

EXEGETICAL ISSUES

Modern readers find this passage difficult to understand and reflect on for several reasons. The *episkopos*, often translated as "bishop," is not the citywide Church leader we associate with that term, but seems rather to lead a relatively small local community; to avoid anachronism, the word is translated here as "overseer," which is literally what the word means in Greek, but is not the title of a Church office known to us today. The treatment of the overseer and deacons is not a functional job description, as we would like and expect, but instead comes in the form of virtue and vice lists. These are unfamiliar to us, though a common-enough treatment in antiquity for treating moral character or the requirements for office.[2] Indeed, these virtue and vice lists, understood (in the way we tend to do) as job qualifications rather than norms to be sought, would make any self-aware applicant today feel woefully unfit for either office. In particular, our more individualistic self-understanding tends to recoil at the idea that fitness for office should depend on the conduct of one's spouse and children (3:4–5, 12). Moreover, for those seeking a direct pattern for the qualifications of bishops and deacons today, that of stability in marriage (3:2, 12)[3] and experience managing a household (3:4–5, 12) obviously will not apply to a bishop, and even if applied to married deacons, this norm would be expressed today in a less authoritarian way. The sudden, brief mention of women (3:11) in the section on deacons, who are otherwise presented as male, suggests the currently debated matter of ordaining women to the diaconate, but without providing any clarification, owing to the brevity of the individual verse and the difficulty of interpreting what it actually means.[4] To engage 1 Timothy 3:1–13 correctly, one must lay aside today's particular cultural and ecclesiastical preconceptions. Still, the situation the letter addresses certainly has analogies to life in the Church today: the letter's context is a community torn apart by conflicts about teaching and morality. The overseer and deacons are being exhorted to exemplify sound faith and unimpeachable morality as a help in overcoming these conflicts.[5]

TASKS AND FUNCTIONS

If read carefully, the virtue and vice lists do offer some indications about the functions of the overseer and deacons, although as we noted in chapter 2 the passage particularly stresses their collaboration. The most remarkable characteristic of these two moral portraits is how similar they are, how parallel are the lists of virtues and vices, the qualities themselves, and even the number listed. A full exegesis of this artfully constructed text is beyond our scope here, but the parallel structure is clear in a careful reading of the passage itself.[6] The overseer and the deacons are similar in their characters (the repeated virtues/vices), in their self-presentation (serious, self-controlled, respectable), and in their social/familial location (heads of households). A close collaboration between the two offices is expressed rhetorically in the passage by the strong parallel between the moral characters they are exhorted to exemplify; we can conclude that the deacons have a collaborative and assisting role with respect to the overseer's functions.

Precisely because the similarities are so marked, some particular qualifications for each office emerge from an attentive comparison. This can begin with the names of the offices: *episkopos* literally means an overseer, and a *diakonos* is some kind of assistant, or a person who acts for another. The single overseer has more than one deacon. In general terms, then, the functional roles are suggested by the titles. More specifically, the overseer's office requires the exercise of hospitality (3:2), which presumably would include oversight of community gatherings. He also should be able to teach (3:2), and he seems to have primary responsibility for dealing with outsiders (3:7). Neither the overseer nor the deacons should be greedy (3:3, 8), an emphasis that suggests they both have responsibility for the community goods and funds, which, as the community certainly gathered for meals, would include food.

The specific functions of the deacons are less distinct, as we would expect of someone who assists or acts on behalf of the overseer and takes on an implementing role with respect to some of the overseer's functions. The strong faith and trustworthiness (3:9, 11, 13) to which deacons are exhorted particularly are valuable for assistants to or agents for someone else. The deacons' culminating virtue, translated here as "confidence," is *parrhesia* (3:13), which includes as a primary meaning the ability to speak frankly and boldly. This suggests a role for deacons keeping order in assemblies that could become unruly (2:8; 6:3-5). Taking together the overseer's various functions and the assisting role of the deacon, as well as the indications of specific roles with community funds and keeping order, then the office of deacon appears as a stable ministry with multiple functions in its early Church context.

APPENDIX THREE

• • • • • • •

JOHN N. COLLINS AND THE "DEACON WORDS"

Chapter 8 showed a coherence, discovered through a theological reflection on Scripture, among the four aspects of Christ the servant, effectively combining them into a single metaphor that illuminates one dimension of the person and activity of Christ. What does not hold the different aspects of this image together is a common participation in any word or word group. This may seem to be a rather abstract methodological point, but it is important because words and their range of meaning are the basis of John N. Collins's influential critique of Christ the servant as a model for diaconal ministry. Chapter 8 engages that critique directly, but to clarify Collins's reasoning it is useful to distinguish more precisely between a theological understanding of Christ the servant and the kind of understanding Collins favors, which is reached by considering the range of meaning for particular words (lexical domains). Chapter 8 shows that the image of Christ the servant *need not* fit into the lexical domain of the *diakon-* words in order to be a fruitful and indeed foundational model for the modern diaconate. This appendix reviews the several lexical domains closest to the metaphor of Christ the servant and shows that no one lexical domain *can* capture this image in full, precisely because its coherence is conceptual rather than lexical.

THE *SERV-* AND MINISTRY WORDS

Although we are aided in formulating the metaphor of Christ the servant by the umbrella of the *serv-* words (servant/ serve/service), there are areas of meaning within the *serv-* words that do not apply to Christ, especially the sense of *servile* as the inner characteristic of being cringing, weak, or unfree. More- over, for aspects of Christ the servant there are other words that express its meaning as well or better than the *serv-* words. An obvious one is the *minister—ministry* group, which expresses the idea of undertaking a task under the direction of, or as agent for, someone else. These words apply as well or better than the *serv-* words to Christ's relation to the Father (the dimen- sion "whose servant?") and to Christ in his mission of salvation ("serving whom?"), especially as the ministry words avoid even the hint of servility. Thus, the *serv-* words help us make an anal- ogy between a phenomenon in human social relations and one aspect of Christ's person and activity, but our understanding of Christ the servant is not captured within the boundaries of meaning for those words.

THE GREEK WORDS:
DIAKON-, *DOUL-*, AND *PAIS*.

More central to Collins's argument is the view that key aspects of the image of Christ the servant are not captured by the *diakon-* words, including *diakonos* and *diakonia*. Collins's exhaustive word study of 1990 concluded that the *diakon-* words actually refer to being sent out or acting on behalf of someone else, and have nothing to do with charity and humble service, which are constituent elements of the metaphor of Christ the servant.[1] Collins's evidence was conclusive and resulted in a change in the leading dictionary of New Testament and early Christian Greek.[2] His translation of the *diakon-* words has been followed throughout this book.

Nevertheless, we can speak, as Polycarp did (and as *Lumen Gentium* 29 quoted him) of "Christ the *diakonos*," and see, at

151

least in part, the image of Christ the servant. But our theological understanding of that dimension of Christ is no more captured by the *diakon-* words than by the *serv-* words. The text of Scripture itself supports this conclusion. The various aspects of servanthood in the image of Christ the servant do not depend on a single word group, but draw on three different Greek words (*diakonos, doulos,* and *pais*). These words, found in the New Testament and in the Septuagint, the Greek translation of the Old Testament, have overlapping meanings. All three word groups denote servanthood of some kind; their precise meaning depends on the context.[3]

In fact, all three Greek words in Scripture contribute to the understanding of servanthood in the image of Christ the servant as developed through its four aspects in chapter 8. The Greek *diakon-* words themselves actually refer best only to our first two aspects of Christ the servant as a model for deacons, "whose servant?" and "serving whom?": deacons serve the bishop, the faithful, and the Church's mission in the world. The focus on humble service in Christ the servant is better captured by the Greek *doul-* words that express the condition and activity of servitude/servanthood that the New Testament applied both to Christ and to ministers of the gospel, as well as to ordinary servants and slaves.[4] Considered from the viewpoint of word definitions, then, *Lumen Gentium* 29 moved partway out of the *diakon-*words into the sphere of the *doul-* words in applying the image of Christ the servant to the revived diaconate.

The metaphor of Christ the servant, then, is not constrained by any particular group of words. Specifically, it is not possible to tie this image to diaconal ministry through the meanings of the Greek words *diakonos* and *diakonia*. As considered theologically in chapter 8, however, this metaphor does provide a valid, scripturally grounded, and coherent perspective on Christ's person and saving activity. This metaphor, moreover, becomes a fruitful model for the modern diaconate, beginning with the seed from Polycarp in *Lumen Gentium* 29.

NOTES

CHAPTER ONE

1. For the inauguration of the diaconate see Paul VI, *motu proprio Sacrum Diaconatus Ordinem* (June 18, 1967), in *Acta Apostolicae Sedis* [hereafter *AAS*] 59 (1967): 697–704. For worldwide diaconate statistics, see *Statistical Yearbook of the Church 2016* (Vatican City: Typis Polyglottis, 2018), 92–100, giving statistics as of December 31, 2016. The number in the text includes diocesan deacons only. These comprise the vast majority and certainly the typical case.

2. Per the *Statistical Yearbook 2016*, 94–95, the three countries outside Western Europe and North America with significant numbers of diocesan deacons are Brazil (4,424), Chile (1,113), and Mexico (1,066).

3. The question of whether women should be ordained to the diaconate has received a fair degree of coverage in the general media, but this topic excites interest as part of the wider discussion about the role of women in the Catholic Church, rather than because of any particular focus on diaconal ministry.

4. See Tim O'Donnell, "Should Deacons Represent Christ the Servant?" *Theological Studies* 78, no. 4 (2017): 850–78, and further in this book, esp. chaps. 3, 5, 7, and 8, where the content of this article is expanded and developed.

5. Vatican Council II, Constitution on the Church *Lumen Gentium* (November 21, 1964) [hereafter *LG*] 29, in Norman P. Tanner, ed., *Decrees of the Ecumenical Councils*, 2 vols. (Washington, DC: Georgetown University Press, 1989), 2:874 (hereafter cited as Tanner). There is ongoing ambiguity about whether or in what way leadership of some kind is an intrinsically diaconal task; see chap. 7 below.

6. The writings with a practical focus include descriptions of the diaconate on diocesan websites, books and magazine articles about the

experiences of deacons in ministry, diocesan handbooks and directories, reflections on diaconal roles in particular ministries and contexts, and retreat guides. Examples will be cited in the following chapters.

7. The theological treatments include numerous journal articles and collections of article-length pieces, but many fewer book-length treatments by a single author; of these longer arguments, none lays out a complete definition of diaconal identity that is both theologically coherent and practically useful—the goal of this book. There will be many citations below.

8. For examples of longer treatments with a significant focus on diaconal identity but coming to very general or tentative conclusions, see International Theological Commission (ITC), *Le diaconat: evolution et perspectives (2003)* (http://www.vatican.va/roman _curia/congregations/cfaith/cti_documents/rc_con_cfaith_pro _05072004_diaconate_fr.html), esp. the concluding section; unofficial English translation (hereafter E.T.), *From the Diakonia of Christ to the Diakonia of the Apostles* (Chicago: Hillebrand, 2003), 91–110; William T. Ditewig, *The Emerging Diaconate: Servant Leaders in a Servant Church* (New York: Paulist Press, 2007), which proposes ten useful "points of reference" for a theology of the diaconate (123–43) and concludes with "emerging challenges" (197–219); Kenan B. Osborne, *The Permanent Diaconate: Its History and Place in the Sacrament of Orders* (New York: Paulist Press, 2007), esp. 136–40, 147–53; and Alphonse Borras, *Le diaconat au risque de sa nouveauté* (Brussels: Lessius, 2007), broad conclusions at 206–15.

9. Some of the more theologically developed but also speculative treatments of diaconal identity have been coming from Germany: see Christian Wesseley, *Gekommen, um zu dienen. Der Diakonat aus fundamentaltheologisch-ekklesiologischer Sicht* (Regensburg: Friedrich Pustet, 2004), esp. 223–25, on deacons occupying a "borderland" between secularity and holiness; Hans-Joachim Sander, "Diakonat: die heterotope Dimension des kirchlichen Amtes," in *Ortsbestimmungen: Der Diakonat als kirchlicher Dienst*, ed. Richard Hartmann, Franz Reger, and Stefan Sander (Frankfurt am Main: Josef Knecht, 2009), 38–58, on the "heterotopic" location of deacons; and Stefan Sander, *Gott begegnet im Anderen. Der Diakon und die Einheit des sakramentalen Amtes* (Freiburg: Herder, 2006), 261–304, on the deacon's identification with "the other." As accounts of the diaconal identity, these treatments are best understood as developments in the more deeply rooted understanding of the deacon as minister of the threshold, developed in chap. 9 below.

10. The ITC, in *Le diaconat*, section 6 (E.T., 79–90), provides a useful survey of the worldwide diaconate in two "typical cases," North

America/Western Europe and the rest of the world. However, the ITC does not integrate this practical context into its theological treatment of diaconal ministry (concluding section, E.T., 91–110).

11. See, e.g., Thomas F. O'Meara, *Theology of Ministry*, 2nd ed. (New York: Paulist Press, 1999), esp. 5–138; and Kenan B. Osborne, *Orders and Ministry: Leadership in the World Church* (New York: Orbis Books, 2006).

12. The Anglicans, Orthodox, and Eastern Catholics all have transitional as well as permanent diaconates. The specifically Roman Catholic focus here differs from that of the influential writings of John N. Collins, whose work will be engaged below; he studies the diaconate in all the Christian denominations as a single phenomenon with a variety of subthemes. See, e.g., his *Deacons and the Church: Making Connections between Old and New* (Harrisburg, PA: Morehouse, 2002), "written for deacons of any denomination" (vii).

13. As of December 31, 2016, 73.3 percent of the 45,609 diocesan permanent deacons worldwide were from North America and Europe, 43 percent in North America alone (*Statistical Yearbook of the Church 2016*, 92–100). The heavy numerical preponderance of the diaconate in these countries, together with the concentration of theological study centers in them, has resulted in a near-total concentration in the theological literature (whether tacit or openly stated) on this social and ecclesial context. Moreover, as deacons are scattered broadly and unevenly over the rest of the world, there is no other numerically significant typical context to address.

14. This first condition, addressing the ecclesial context for diaconal development, was proposed by William T. Ditewig, "The Once and Future Diaconate: Notes from the Past, Possibilities for the Future," *Church* 20, no. 1 (2004): 51–54.

CHAPTER TWO

1. For a summary of the ancient ordination rites for deacons, see Paul F. Bradshaw, *Ordination Rites of the Ancient Churches of East and West* (New York: Pueblo, 1990), 71–82, referencing English translations of the rites included in that volume. In mid-twentieth century scholarship, *Apostolic Tradition* carried particular authority among historians of the diaconate because it was believed to describe Roman practice in the early third century. Recently, a more complicated textual history has been proposed. See Paul F. Bradshaw, Maxwell E.

Johnson, and L. Edward Phillips, *The Apostolic Tradition: A Commentary*, Hermeneia (Minneapolis: Fortress Press, 2002), 1–17 on the text, 60–64 for diaconal ordination. Alistair Stewart argues for a retrievable text with an early third-century date and Roman context, but he sees the ordination rites as idealized rather than descriptive of actual practice. See his Hippolytus, *On the Apostolic Tradition: An English Version with Introduction and Commentary*, 2nd ed., Popular Patristics Series (Yonkers, NY: St. Vladimir Seminary Press, 2015), 15–64 on the text, 102–8 on diaconal ordination.

2. In the diaconate literature, James Monroe Barnet, *The Diaconate: A Full and Equal Order*, 2nd ed. (Harrisburg, PA: Trinity International, 1995), 3–128; ITC, *Le diaconat*, section 1 (E.T., 3–44); Stefan Sander, *Das Amt des Diakons*, 2nd ed. (Freiburg im Breisgau: Herder, 2008), 19–99; John N. Collins, *Deacons and the Church: Making Connections between Old and New* (Harrisburg, PA: Morehouse, 2002), 86–117.

3. Recent studies with extensive references: Alistair Stewart, *The Original Bishops* (Grand Rapids: Baker Academic, 2014), 100–19; Alexandre Faivre, "La question des ministères à l'époque paléochrétienne, problématiques et enjeux d'une périodisation," in *Les Pères de l'Église et les ministères: évolutions, idéal et réalités: actes du IIIe colloque de La Rochelle, 7, 8 et 9 septembre 2007*, ed. Pascal-Grégoire Delage (La Rochelle: Association Histoire et Culture, 2008), 3–38.

4. *LG* 29, Tanner, 2:874, lines 26–27: "the diaconate can in the future be restored as a distinct and permanent grade of the hierarchy."

5. For a broad view of *ressourcement* and its contribution to the council, see John W. O'Malley, *What Happened at Vatican II* (Cambridge, MA: Harvard University Press, 2006), 40–43, 75–76, 300–303.

6. See Jean Lécuyer, "Diaconat," *Dictionnaire de spiritualité: ascétique et mystique, doctrine et histoire*, 17 vols in 20 (Paris: Beauchesne, 1932–1995), 3:799–803 (published 1958); Jean Colson, "Der Diakonat im Neuen Testament" and "Diakon und Bischof in den ersten drei Jahrhunderten der Kirche;" and Walter Croce, "Aus der Geschichte des Diakonats," in *Diaconia in Christo. Über die Erneuerung des Diakonates*, ed. Karl Rahner and Herbert Vorgrimler, Quaestiones Disputatae 15/16 (Freiburg: Herder, 1962) [hereafter *Diaconia in Christo*], summarizing their work from the 1950s.

7. The ancient Church sources describing ordination rites for deacons gave historical support for seeing deacons as ordained ministers, although the medieval expansion of clerical orders (including, e.g., subdeacon, acolyte, lector, and porter), together with the diaconate's loss of a distinct ministerial function, contributed to some uncertainty

in modern Catholic thought about whether deacons were still in the major orders along with bishops and priests. See chap. 3 below.

8. For a brief treatment with references, Anthony Barrett, "What Is Ordination? A Roman Catholic Perspective," *Ecclesiology* 3 (2006): 66–70.

9. Because the council's restoration did not consider the possibility of women deacons, and accordingly relied on ancient precedents for male deacons, the more recent debate about whether to ordain women to the diaconate is very concerned with evaluating early Church models for this practice. Should the Church decide to allow ordination of women to the diaconate, the ministerial identity for which they would be commissioned would be that developed since Vatican II, an identity that, based on the two models developed in this book, is not gender specific. See chap. 7.

10. The method adopted here specifically focuses on "the world of the text" and "the world before the text" as formulated by Sandra M. Schneiders, *The Revelatory Text* (New York: HarperCollins, 1991), 132–90.

11. We are following the text itself here, and not engaging the question raised by historical criticism, whether the commissioning for the Twelve had primarily an eschatological import rather than a focus on leadership and mission.

12. The following passages, while hardly exhaustive, are illustrative: Jesus commissions the Twelve, Mark 6:7–13/Matt 10:1–15/Luke 9:1–6; the eleven, Matt 28:16–20/Mark 16:14–18; and the Seventy, Luke 10:1–12. Appointment of the Seven: Acts 6:1–6; diversity of ministries in the Pauline churches: 1 Cor 12:4–31, Rom 12:6–8, Eph 4:11 (see also 1 Pet 4:10–11); *episkopoi* and *diakonoi*: 1 Tim 3:1–13; apostles, James, and elders, Acts 14:23, 15, 1 Pet 5:1–2, Jas 5:14; Timothy as an apostolic delegate commissioned by Paul and elders, 1 Tim 4:11–16; Titus as an apostolic delegate appointing elders, Titus 1:5.

13. Roman Catholic interpreters of Acts 6:1–6 have been drawn to the view that the Seven were the first deacons out of respect for that interpretation in Tradition, and because this view is one way of rooting the diaconate in the divine institution of holy orders, from Christ through the apostles. The argument for divine institution does not require this particular interpretation of Acts 6:1–6, however: see, e.g., Gerhard Müller, "The Sacramental Diaconate," in *Priesthood and Diaconate: The Recipient of Holy Orders from the Perspective of Creation Theology and Eschatology*, trans. Michael J. Miller (San Francisco: Ignatius Press, 2000), 183–203, esp. 194–95. Nor is a specifically Roman Catholic exegesis required to identify the Seven with deacons: see P. Gaechter, "Die Sieben," *Zeitschrift für Katholische Theologie* 74 (1952): 129–66, which concludes

that they were *episkopoi*. This article carried significant weight with the preconciliar historians and theologians supporting a revival of the diaconate: citing Gaechter, they avoided appeals to Acts 6:1–6 as a foundation story. The Protestant Reformers in the sixteenth century continued the tradition of interpreting Acts 6:1–6 as the appointment of deacons: see the extracts collected in Esther Chung-Kim and Todd R. Hains, eds., *Reformation Commentary on Scripture*, New Testament VI, *Acts* (Downers Grove, IL: IVP Academic, 2014), 71–77. Thus, this text retained a defining authority for the office of deacon, which was developed widely and took on added importance in the Protestant churches, generally with a focus on church administration and social welfare. See Jeanine Olson, *Deacons and Deaconesses through the Centuries*, 2nd ed. (St. Louis: Concordia, 2005), 107–378.

14. "Your Son's Apostles appointed seven men of good repute to assist them in the daily ministry." See *Rites of Ordination of a Bishop, of Priests, and of Deacons*, Second Typical Edition (Washington, DC: United States Conference of Catholic Bishops, 2002), 129.

15. Some but not all of the ancient consecratory prayers incorporate the model of the Seven or of Stephen. See Bradshaw, *Ordination Rites of the Ancient Churches*, 72–80, with references to the texts of the various prayers in English translation, included in the same volume. The Seven and Stephen in these prayers are general models of holiness and zeal.

16. Two other New Testament mentions of *diakonoi* may well refer to deacons (Rom 16:1; Phil 1:1), but could be referring only in a general way to people who are serving the churches or helping with Paul's mission. Even if these texts do refer to deacons, the mentions are too brief to tell us anything substantive about their office.

17. See Tim O'Donnell, "The Rhetorical Strategy of 1 Timothy," *Catholic Biblical Quarterly* 79, no. 3 (2017): 255–75. The interpretation offered in this chapter does not depend on a particular dating of 1 Tim or whether Paul was in fact the author; see the article just cited at 458, with references.

18. Stewart, *The Original Bishops*, 100–19.

19. An influential historical reconstruction has pictured a unitary movement from an early charismatic Church reflected in 1 Cor to an ecclesiastical one ("early Catholicism") dominated by officeholders, reflected, e.g., in 1 Tim. For a recent, vigorous critique of this narrative, see Benjamin L. White, "The Traditional and Ecclesiastical Paul of 1 Corinthians," *Catholic Biblical Quarterly* 79, no. 4 (2017): 651–69.

20. The inclusion of *diakonia* among the spiritual gifts in Rom 12:8 (not in 1 Cor 12:1–4 or Eph 4:11) uses a general word for service

or ministry of various kinds; there is no reason to connect it with the office of deacon.

21. Paul F. Bradshaw, *Rites of Ordination: Their History and Theology* (Collegeville, MN: The Liturgical Press, 2013), 17–38, provides an excellent brief account, with references.

22. This view of the diaconate as an office that should inspire or be a vehicle for multiple charisms contrasts usefully with profession in religious communities, which often seek to be a vehicle for a particular charism.

23. 1 Cor 12:12–27; Rom 12:4–8; Eph 4:12.

24. On the relational pattern running through 1 Tim, see O'Donnell, "Rhetorical Strategy," esp. 464–70.

25. On the function and structuring of personal examples in this letter, see O'Donnell, "Rhetorical Strategy," 464–75. More broadly, Abraham J. Malherbe, *Moral Exhortation: A Greco-Roman Sourcebook*, Library of Early Christianity (Philadelphia: Westminster, 1986), 135–38; and Benjamin Fiore, *The Function of Personal Example in the Socratic and Pastoral Epistles*, Analecta Biblica 105 (Rome: Biblical Institute Press, 1986), esp. 45–163.

26. On the dysfunction of "exemplarism," (the need to project moral and spiritual perfection), see Owen F. Cummings, *Deacons and the Church* (New York: Paulist Press, 2004), 111–13.

27. Texts in Bart Ehrmann, ed., *The Apostolic Fathers*, 2 vols., Loeb Classical Library (Cambridge, MA: Harvard University Press, 2003) 1:201–354.

28. Polycarp, *Philippians* 5.2; 1 Tim 3:8–13.

29. *Philippians* 5.2.

30. Ignatius, *Philadelphians*, prologue.

31. Ignatius, *Magnesians* 6.1; *Trallians* 3.1.

32. Ignatius, *Magnesians* 13.2, *Smyrnaeans* 8.1–3.

33. *Trallians* 2.3

34. The theme is seen most clearly in the *Apostolic Tradition* and the *Testamentum Domini*. For the texts, see Bradshaw, Johnson, and Phillips, *The Apostolic Tradition*, 60–61. For the current ordination prayer, see *Rites of Ordination*, 130.

CHAPTER THREE

1. Council of Trent, Session XXIII, July 15, 1563, does not make a clear distinction between major and minor orders. Chap. 4 speaks of

"the ordination of bishops, priests, and other orders" (Tanner, 2:743, lines 16–17). Canon 6 speaks of a "hierarchy consisting of bishops, priests, and ministers" (Tanner, 2:744, lines 8–9).

2. Canon 17, Tanner, 2:750, lines 15–16.

3. Canon 2: "If anyone says that, aside from the priesthood, there do not exist other orders, both major and minor, in the Catholic Church, by which the priesthood is reached by successive steps: let him be anathema." Tanner, 2:743, lines 35–37.

4. Pius XII, *Sacramentum Ordinis*, November 30, 1947, http://w2.vatican.va/content/pius-xii/la/apost_constitutions/documents/hf_p-xii_apc_19471130_sacramentum-ordinis.html.

5. The articles on the diaconate in the Greek, Slavic, Orthodox, and Eastern Catholic Churches in *Diaconia in Christo*, 136–99, implicitly ask precisely this question. This six hundred–page collection of articles, published on the eve of the council and making a case for a renewed diaconate, will be discussed below in this chapter.

6. Jeanine Olson, *Deacons and Deaconesses through the Centuries*, 2nd ed. (St. Louis: Concordia, 2005), 107–378.

7. Olson, *Deacons and Deaconesses*, 209–10; Herbert Krimm, "Der Diakon in den evangelischen Kirchen," in *Diaconia in Christo*, 198, reports, among Protestants, 15 Brother Houses and 4,550 deacons and candidates in Germany in 1962.

8. For a dictionary definition of *Diakonie* as service to the needy, see https://www.duden.de/rechtschreibung/Diakonie (accessed April 3, 2020). John N. Collins has shown that this meaning is incorrect as a translation of the Greek *diakonia* (see chap. 8 below), but *Diakonie* by now is a German word with its own meaning, not merely a translation.

9. See Tim O'Donnell, "How the Ecclesiological Visions of Vatican II Framed the Ministry of Permanent Deacons," *Worship* 85, no. 5 (2011): 425–46. Much of this chapter is an expansion of that article.

10. Margaret Morche, *Zur Erneuerung des Ständigen Diakonats* (Freiburg: Lambertus, 1996), 15–62, 209–27; Joseph Hornef and Paul Winninger, "Chronique de la restauration du diaconat (1945–1965)," in *Le Diacre dans l'Église et dans le monde d'aujourd'hui*, ed. Paul Winninger and Yves Congar, Unam Sanctam 59 (Paris: Cerf, 1966), 207–8. (Volume hereafter cited as *Diacre*.)

11. Otto Pies, "Block 26: Erfahrungen aus dem Priesterleben in Dachau," *Stimmen der Zeit* 141 (1947–48): 10–28.

12. Hornef and Winninger in *Diacre*, 205–207.

13. The contributions published in 1962 covering Latin America, Africa, Indonesia, and India in *Diaconia in Christo*, 463–515, 540–47,

sum up a range of publications from the previous ten years.

14. The German activists and theologians made particular use of the journals *Der Seelsorger* and *Caritas*. French articles appeared in the *Nouvelle revue théologique* and a variety of publications devoted to parish life. European-based journals devoted to the missions and issued in all the major languages addressed the possibility of the diaconate in the churches outside Europe and North America. See the bibliography in *Diaconia in Christo*, 621–30.

15. Willem van Bekkum, "The Liturgical Revival in Service of the Missions," in *The Assisi Papers: Proceedings of the First International Conference of Pastoral Liturgy, Assisi-Rome, September 18–22, 1956* (Collegeville, MN: The Liturgical Press, 1957), 110–11; Johannes Hofinger, "Permanent Deacons in the Missions," in *Liturgy and the Missions: The Nijmegen Papers*, ed. J. Hofinger (New York: P. J. Kenedy & Sons, 1957), 177–90.

16. The question of ordaining women to the diaconate, or of reviving the office of deaconess from the early Church, was simply not part of the discussion either before or during Vatican II. Defining his aim in the 1962 essay "Theology of the Restoration of the Diaconate," Rahner wrote, "The only problem concerning us here is to determine to whom in the Church it makes any sense to give that sacrament which already exists at the present time and which as such is given to men only." See *Theological Investigations*, trans. Cornelius Ernst (New York: Seabury, 1966) 5:283. (This is a translation of his article in *Diaconia in Christo*, 285–324.) Rahner defines the question narrowly so as to minimize the proposed change and thereby seek broad support for it. On the other hand, his primary rationale for the diaconate, that the Church should strengthen with sacramental grace those laypeople already doing diaconal work ("anonymous deacons"—"Theology of the Restoration," 283), certainly implies that such grace should be bestowed on anyone doing that work, women as well as men. This implication was noted by one of the opponents as a reason why that rationale was inadmissible: Robert Rouquette, "Vers un renouveau du diaconat?" *Études* 301 (1959): 240. The "anonymous deacon" rationale for a permanent diaconate is absent from *LG* 29, but appears in *Ad Gentes* 16, Tanner 2:1026, lines 8–13, which refers to "men [*viros*] who are already exercising what is really a deacon's ministry."

17. Michel. D. Epagneul, "Du rôle du diacre dans l'église d'aujourd'hui," *Nouvelle revue théologique* 79 (1957): 153–68. Epagneul was the founder of the Missionary Brothers of the Countryside.

18. "Quelques aspects fondamentaux de l'apostolat des laïcs," *AAS* 49 (1957): 925.

19. Hornef and Winninger in *Diacre*, 213, referring to Winninger's *Vers un renouveau du diaconat* (Paris: Desclée de Brouwer, 1958). The heightened official concern about a married diaconate is shown by a comparison with a work published five years earlier, Wilhelm Schamoni's *Married Men as Ordained Deacons* (London: Burns & Oates, 1955; German original, 1953), which did receive the imprimatur.

20. Rahner wrote to Vorgrimler on May 9, 1962, "The book is gigantic. Are 620 pages still not the end? What kind of serious studies have appeared for the Council? I know of nothing except this book." Herbert Vorgrimler, *Understanding Karl Rahner* (New York: Crossroad, 1986), 147.

21. The best survey of preconciliar writings on the diaconate is Piercarlo Beltrando, *Diaconi per la Chiesa. Itinerario ecclesiologico del Ripristino del Ministero diaconale* (Milan: Istituto Propaganda, 1977), 19-150. For the way the debate was rooted in ideas about the clergy and the Church, see O'Donnell, "Ecclesiological Visions," 425-32.

22. Representative of the viewpoints of the opponents: Rouquette, "Vers un renouveau du diaconat?"; Giuseppe Rambaldi, "Forme Diverse di un Immutabile ed Unico Sacerdozio," *Civiltà Cattolica* 111, no. 4 (1960): 27-40; H. Holstein, "Vers une restauration du diaconat?" *Études* 306 (1960): 256-63. The schematic presentation in this section differs from the sources in two ways. First, the opponents often write more tentatively than this account suggests. Except on the issue of celibacy, where they tend to be quite definite, their tone is one of caution rather than militancy. But their views are clear enough. Second, because of the relative scarcity of published writings by the opponents, the opposing views have been fleshed out to some extent by giving lines of reasoning against which the supporters of the diaconate seem to be arguing.

23. The proponents' writings are voluminous. See especially *Diaconia in Christo*, passim, and especially articles by Rahner, Kerkwoorde, Lécuyer, and Lepargneur. The major contributors had published numerous articles and some monographs on their subjects during the 1950s; see the bibliography at *Diaconia in Christo*, 621-34. Also: Schamoni, *Married Men as Ordained Deacons*; Winninger, *Vers un renouveau du diaconat*; Paul Winninger and Joseph Hornef, "Le renouveau du diaconat. Situation présente de la controverse," *Nouvelle revue théologique* 83 (1961): 337-66.

24. On the priest shortage in France and West Germany, in absolute numbers and in geographical distribution: Winninger, *Vers un renouveau du diaconat*, 17-21.

25. In 1959, Msgr. J. Rodhain penned a public letter to the superior of a major seminary in France, considering the diaconate from the viewpoint of vocations, and concluding that there was a nonpriestly ministerial role, focused mainly on service to the poor and parish administration, for which there were numerous authentic vocations. He envisioned deacons and priests as the two complementary arms of a bishop's ministry and argued that "the priesthood will die unless the diaconate is rehabilitated." Quote, summary, and discussion in Beltrando, *Diaconi per la Chiesa*, 75–77.

26. Rahner, "Theology of the Restoration," 283.

27. For example, Yves Congar, *Jalons pour une théologie du laicat* (Paris: 1953), 313, stresses the close connection of Christian charity with the Eucharist, and concludes that "the work of Christian charity...may not in itself be a totally lay activity." Quoted in Beltrando, *Diaconi per la Chiesa*, 59.

28. "The deacon, who belongs theologically and canonically to the clergy—the hierarchy—but is counted psychologically and culturally among the laity or people, becomes a fortunate place of mediation." Francois Lepargneur, "Ein Diakonat für Lateinamerika" in *Diaconia in Christo*, 476.

29. Hannes Kramer, "Die liturgischen Dienste des Diakons" in *Diakonia in Christo*, 367–68.

CHAPTER FOUR

1. The Council's Decree on the Eastern Catholic Churches *Orientalium Ecclesiarum* (November 21, 1964), no. 17, provides a strong charter for the revival of the diaconate in those churches by providing that "the institution of the permanent diaconate should be restored where it has fallen into disuse" (Tanner, 2:905, lines 2–3). This revival is not just an option given to episcopal/eparchial conferences, as will be the case in the Western Church. Given their grounding in ecclesiastical usages that are different from those in the West, the question of ministerial identity (or identities?) for these diaconates has not been addressed in this book, which focuses on the Western diaconate, which received its charter from *LG* 29 and *AG* 16.

2. The interpretive approach used in chaps. 4–6 recognizes the fierce debate over the interpretation of the council, between emphases on continuity with the Church's tradition and on reform/renewal in accord with "the signs of the times," as well described by Massimo

Faggioli, *Vatican II: The Battle for Meaning* (New York: Paulist Press, 2012). The final content of *LG* 29 shows the attempt to balance and compromise between these two pulls. The history of the debate and the reading of *LG* 29 in this chapter uses the "authorial" approach identified by Ormond Rush, *Still Interpreting Vatican II: Some Hermeneutical Principles* (New York: Paulist Press, 2004). Two other approaches he identifies—textual and intertextual—are followed in chap. 5, with some additional authorial input based on the drafter's commentary and the *Relatio*. Ormond's fourth approach (reception) is undertaken in chap. 6, where we trace the appropriation and development of *LG* 29's theme of Christ the servant.

3. The opponents' organizational focus was the *Coetus Internationalis Patrum* (the International Group of Fathers), eventually including about three hundred council participants. See Melissa J. Wilde, *Vatican II: A Sociological Analysis of Religious Change* (Princeton, NJ: Princeton University Press, 2007), 61–75.

4. On the Antepreparatory and Preparatory stages, Étienne Fouilloux in Giuseppe Alberigo and Joseph A. Komonchak, eds., *History of Vatican II*, 5 vols. (Leuven: Peeters, 2003), 1:90–166; Piercarlo Beltrando, *Diaconi per la Chiesa. Itinerario ecclesiologico del Ripristino del Ministero diaconale* (Milan: Istituto Propaganda, 1977), 151–62; William T. Ditewig, *The Emerging Diaconate: Servant Leaders in a Servant Church* (New York: Paulist Press, 2007), 102–9.

5. A schema on the sacraments had included a proposal for a renewed diaconate but was tabled in committee. See Komonchak in *History of Vatican II*, 1:187–89.

6. This is version 1 in Giuseppe Alberigo and Franca Magistretti, *Constitutionis Dogmaticae Lumen Gentium Synopsis Historica* (Bologna: Istituto per le Scienze Religiose, 1975), 3–340. (Hereafter cited as *Synopsis*).

7. *Acta Synodalia Sacrosancti Concilii Vaticani II*, 32 vols. (Vatican City: Typis Polyglottis, 1970–1999) I/1:166–75. (Hereafter *AS*) E.T. of this important address by Joseph Komonchak at https://jakomonchak.files.wordpress.com/2012/10/john-xxiii-opening-speech.pdf.

8. Rival versions: *Synopsis*, 361–428.

9. Herbert Vorgrimler, *Understanding Karl Rahner* (New York: Crossroad, 1986), 167–68, with three letters of response. Beltrando, *Diaconi per la Chiesa*, 147–48, noting that *Diaconia in Christo*'s thirty-nine articles by thirty-two authors expressed a wide variety of viewpoints (though all favorable to the diaconate), suggests that this work supported the diaconate by its size and range, rather than by contributing any theological coherence.

Notes

10. July 18, 1870, Tanner, 2:811–16.

11. *Synopsis*, 160–61, "Version 2ter." Two notes on the translation: "for pastoral reasons" = *pro necessitate curae animarum*; "up to the leaders of the church" = *ad praepositos ecclesiae*.

12. There were 119 addresses during this period (Alberto Melloni in *History of Vatican II*, 3:66), and Vorgrimler reports that seventy fathers spoke about the diaconate (*Commentary on the Documents of Vatican II*, 5 vols. [New York: Herder, 1967], 1:226), but not all of these made the diaconate the primary focus of their speeches.

13. For example, Bishop Franjo Šeper of Zagreb on October 9, *AS* II/2:359.

14. As an exception, see the remarkable intervention by Bishop Maurer quoted in the next chapter.

15. Cardinal Paul Marie André Richaud of Bordeaux on October 9, *AS* II/2:346. Bishop Bernard Yago of Abijan, Ivory Coast, October 10, *AS* II/2:407.

16. Cardinal Leo Joseph Suenens of Malines-Brussels, October 8, *AS* II/2:317 and in a press conference, Giovanni Caprile, ed., *Il Concilio Vaticano II: Cronache del Concilio Vaticano II*, 5 vols. in 6 (Rome: Edizioni "La Civiltà Cattolica," 1966–69), 3:76. Hereafter cited as *Chronache*.

17. On October 7, *AS* II/2:227–28. On Rahner's authorship, see the excerpt of his letter to Herbert Vorgrimler dated October 1, 1963, in Vorgrimler, *Understanding Karl Rahner*, 175.

18. Cardinal Suenens on October 8 in the speech and press conference cited above.

19. October 4, *AS* II/2:83.

20. Bishop Paul Sani Kleden, SVD, of Den Pasar, Indonesia, and Bishop Marcel Lefèbvre, CSSp, Superior General of the Holy Ghost Fathers, at press conferences, *Chronache*, 3:108.

21. Bishop Vittorio Maria Costantini, OFM Conv., of Sessa Arunca, Italy, October 11, *Chronache*, 3:87.

22. Cardinal Ottaviani, during the debate on the laity, October 21, proposed commissioning acolytes: *Chronache*, 3:125.

23. Archbishop Custódio Alvim Pereira of Lourenco Marques, Mozambique, in the name of twenty-eight Portuguese bishops, October 14, *Chronache*, 3:91. Bishop Paul Zoungrana, MAfr, of Upper Volta, West Africa, October 14, *Chronache*, 3:94.

24. Bishop Petar Čule of Mostar, Yugoslavia, October 14, *Chronache*, 3:92.

25. October 4, *Chronache*, 3:43.

26. Xavier Rynne, *Vatican Council II* (Maryknoll, NY: Orbis Books, 2002), 190–91.

27. Examples: Cardinal Landázuri-Ricketts of Lima, Peru, speaking for thirty-seven Peruvian and fifty-eight other Latin American bishops, October 8, *AS* II/2:314–16; Bishop Maurer of Sucre, Bolivia, for the Bolivian episcopate and twenty others, October 10, *AS* II/2:409–11.

28. For example: supporting married deacons: Bishop Yago of Abijan, Ivory Coast, speaking for forty West African bishops, October 10, *Cronache*, 3:82. Supporting celibacy in general but allowing the pope to lift the requirement if appropriate: Bishop Zoungrana, of Upper Volta, October 14, *AS* II/2:537–39.

29. October 10, *Cronache*, 3:84.

30. *AS* II/2:537.

31. *Synopsis*, 430.

32. Votes in *Chronache*, 3:168. It is notable that opposition to the diaconate proposal exceeded that for all the votes on collegiality, which passed by 80–90 percent margins.

33. The drafting committee report in *Synopsis*, 464–66 gives a good summary of the arguments on both sides.

34. The text of *LG* 29 (see below) acknowledges the lack of a consistent institutional framework among the conferences when it refers to them as "of various kinds." By giving the conferences a distinct task, the council challenged them to become more vital and to take responsibility for the new collegial order in the Church. But whether they would succeed in ordaining deacons where pastoral needs most required them remained an open question.

35. Hilari Raguer in *History of Vatican II*, 2:187–94.

36. The votes are in *Chronache*, 3:107.

37. *Sacrum Diaconatus Ordinem*, June 8, 1967.

38. *Chronache*, 4:108.

39. Pope Benedict XVI, addressing the interpretation of the council, makes a distinction between a "hermeneutic of discontinuity," which he criticizes, and a "hermeneutic of reform," which he deems to be correct. In this hermeneutic, basic principles are affirmed but their expression and application may be new. The interpretation of *LG* 29 presented here fits easily into this "reform hermeneutic" and if anything shows a reluctance to express any discontinuity unless absolutely necessary. See Benedict XVI, *Christmas Address to the Roman Curia*, December 22, 2005 (*AAS* 2006): 45–52. English translation in Matthew L. Lamb and Matthew Levering, *Vatican II: Renewal within Tradition* (New York: Oxford University Press): ix–xv. (hereafter cited as E.T.).

40. *LG* 29, Tanner 2:874, lines 11–34. The phrase "blessings and devotions" translates *sacramentalia*.

41. Useful chart comparing functions in *LG* 29 and in the Code: Ditewig, *Emerging Diaconate*, 90–92.

42. Herbert Vorgrimler, "Liturgie, Diakonie, and Diakone," in *Die Diakonale Dimension der Liturgie*, ed. Benedikt Kraneman, Thomas Sternberg, and Walter Zahner, Quaestiones Disputatae 218 (Freiburg: Herder, 2006), 240–44.

43. Older rite: Apostolic Tradition, see Paul F. Bradshaw, *Ordination Rites of the Ancient Churches of East and West* (New York: Pueblo, 1990), 108. Later rites, see *LG* 29's own citations at Tanner, 2:874n74.

44. The cautious language aimed to avoid outright condemnation of those theologians who denied the sacramentality of the diaconate. See ITC, *Le Diaconat* 4(d) (E.T., 51–58), for discussion of the phrasing in *LG* 29 and the debate after the council about whether the diaconate participates in the sacrament of holy orders.

45. Proposed, e.g., by Archishop Josyf Slipyi of Ukraine, "a sort of social bridge between the community of the faithful and the clergy" *AS* II/2:445. Envisioned in a mission context where priests are scarce, Bishop Paul Yü Pin of Nanjing (*AS* II/2:430–32). Both interventions from October 11, 1963.

46. Both Suenens (*AS* II/2:317) and Döpfner (*AS* II/2:228) argued that the Church should use the sacramental grace of the diaconate to strengthen existing apostolates that were diaconal. This rationale is used in *AG* 16; see chapter 5 below.

CHAPTER FIVE

1. A point noted by Avery Dulles, *Models of the Church*, expanded ed. (New York: Doubleday, 2002), 92, in his treatment of the servant model of the Church.

2. 1 Cor 12:12–26; 1 Pet 2:9–10; Eph 2:19–22; 1 Tim 3:15; the use of *ekklēsia*, "assembly," obviously is widespread in early Christian literature.

3. *AS* I/4:142–44.

4. *LG* 8, Tanner, 2:854, line 31 to 855, line 5.

5. *Gaudium et Spes* 3 (hereafter cited as *GS*), Tanner 2:1070, lines 24–27.

6. *Hodie Concilium* (December 7, 1965) *AAS* 58 (1965): 63. "Servant" here translates *ancillam*.

7. *LG* 18, Tanner, 2:862, lines 35–36. Nathan Mitchell described the importance of this shift, and the contribution of the revived diaconate in effecting it, in *Mission and Ministry: History and Theology*

in the Sacrament of Order (Wilmington, DE: Michael Glazier, 1982), 299–306.

8. Citations for the three tasks are provided below.

9. *AS* II/2:410–11.

10. On the genre and style of the council writings, see John W. O'Malley, *What Happened at Vatican II* (Cambridge, MA: Harvard University Press, 2006), 43–52.

11. *LG* 21, Tanner, 2:865, lines 18–21; *LG* 28, Tanner, 2:872–3.

12. At Tanner, 2:874, line 12.

13. Tanner, 2:874, line 21.

14. *LG* here presents the objective norms and conditions of diaconal activity within the Church, not the inner attitude of service to the people of God, which should characterize bishops and priests as much as deacons.

15. *AS* III/1:260. Discussion in Hervé Legrand, "Le diaconat dans sa relation avec L'Église et ses ministères," in *Diaconat XXIᵉ siècle*, ed. André Hacquin and Phillipe Weber (Brussels: Lumen Vitae, 1997), 23–24. Herbert Vorgrimler, a *peritus* at the council, asserts that *LG* 29 was designed to stress the tasks of social work ("Sozialarbeit") and public witness in the world rather than sacramental and pastoral responsibilities; the list of liturgical and catechetical roles was inserted to help gain the support of Latin American bishops. Herbert Vorgrimler, "Liturgie, Diakonie, and Diakone," in *Die Diakonale Dimension der Liturgie*, ed. Benedikt Kraneman, Thomas Sternberg, and Walter Zahner, Quaestiones Disputatae 218 (Freiburg: Herder, 2006), 240–44.

16. Gérard Philips (*L'Église et son mystère au IIe Concile du Vatican. Histoire, texte, et commentaire de la Constitution Lumen Gentium*, 2 vols. [Paris: Desclée, 1967], 1:376) comments that *diakonos* and *minister* are both generic terms for servant ("serviteur"), and notes that deacons are servants not only of the Church but of priests and bishops.

17. *To the Philippians* 5.2. Polycarp's culminating "servant of all" made his virtue list for deacons more compelling within the framework of a "servant Church" than the virtue lists for deacons in *Didache* 15.1–2 and 1 Tim 3:8–13, which conclude by stressing the honor of the office. Philips (*L'Eglise*, 1:381) notes that the paragraph ends with a return to "charity and administration" and culminates with "Christ, servant of all" in order to provide complete clarity about their paramount significance ("par souci d'exactitude...").

18. *AG* 16, Tanner, 2:1026, lines,. 6–13.

19. The fact of such rivalries during the early centuries was a concern in the preconciliar and conciliar discussions, and is noted with historical references by Philips, *L'Église*, 1:378.

CHAPTER SIX

1. Massimo Faggioli, *Vatican II: The Battle for Meaning* (New York: Paulist Press, 2012), with bibliography. Pope Benedict XVI, *Christmas Address to the Roman Curia*, December 22, 2005 (*AAS* 2006): 45–52 (E.T., ix–xv).

2. *LG* 21, Tanner, 2:865, lines 15–17.

3. See ITC, *Le diaconat*, 7(d)–7(e) (E.T., 51–59).

4. George H. Tavard, *A Theology of Ministry* (Wilmington, DE: Michael Glazier, 1983), 91.

5. In North America (covering the United States and Canada, not Mexico), the number of diocesan priests fell 24 percent from 42,588 in 1978 to 32,200 in 2016. During the same period the number of diocesan priests in Europe fell from 171,351 to 124,948, a loss of 27 percent. In both regions the number of religious order priests fell even more steeply. Taking the two continents in total during the same 1978–2016 period, the number of diocesan permanent deacons rose from 4,525 to 33,965, a jump of 751 percent. *Statistical Yearbook of the Church*: 1987 edition, 77–80, 86–93; 2016 edition, 92–100.

6. For an account of the diaconate's loss of identity by taking on too many "presbyteral roles," see Sherri L. Vallee, "The Restoration of the Permanent Diaconate: A Blending of Roles," *Worship* 77, no. 6 (2003): 530–52.

7. *Ad Pascendum*, *AAS* 64 (1972): 536.

8. This movement, from people to higher clergy, picks up the formula applied to ancient deacons, that they serve as the "eyes and ears of the bishop" (James Monroe Barnet, *The Diaconate: A Full and Equal Order*, 2nd ed. [Harrisburg, PA: Trinity International, 1995], 125), but the two-way movement and "intermediate" condition reflect the twentieth-century discussion about the deacon as a possible bridge figure.

9. Criticized by the ITC, *Le Diaconat*, 7(c) (E.T., 103–4). However, the term is carefully defined in terms of mediating social structures by William S. McKnight, "The Diaconate as *Medius Ordo*: Service in Promotion of Lay Participation," in *The Deacon Reader*, ed. James Keating (New York: Paulist Press, 2006), 78–98, and (in expanded form), W. Shawn McKnight, *Understanding the Diaconate: Historical, Theological, and Sociological Foundations* (Washington, DC: The Catholic University of America Press, 2018), esp. 67–271.

10. Yves Congar, "Le diaconat dans la théologie des ministères" in *Diacre*, 139.

The Deacon

11. Henri Denis, "Le diaconat dans la hiérarchie" in *Diacre*, 148.

12. For an analogous approach, Edward P. Echlin, *The Deacon in the Church: Past and Future* (New York: Alba House, 1971), 127–36, presenting the deacon of the future as "the ordained intermediary of reconciliation," at 136.

13. Discussion with references in ITC, *Le diaconat*, 6(c) (E.T., 84–86).

14. *Le diaconat*, 7(c) (E.T., 104).

15. The ITC's brief discussion at 7(c) primarily concerns the importance of maintaining the lay-clerical distinction, and stressing the different canonical powers given to deacons and priests.

16. Speech to the Italian Diaconate Convention (March 16, 1985), 2, http://w2.vatican.va/content/john-paul-ii/it/speeches/1985/march/documents/hf_jp-ii_spe_19850316_diaconi-permanenti.html.

17. *Catechism of the Catholic Church*, no. 1570, https://www.vatican.va/archive/ENG0015/__P4U.HTM.

18. Congregation for Catholic Education, *Ratio Fundamentalis Institutionum Diaconorum Permanentium* (1998), nos. 5 and 11, http://www.vatican.va/roman_curia/congregations/ccatheduc/documents/rc_con_ccatheduc_doc_31031998_directorium-diaconi_lt.html.

19. *Rites of Ordination of a Bishop, of Priests, and of Deacons*, Second Typical Edition (Washington, DC: United States Conference of Catholic Bishops, 2002), 116.

20. *Rites of Ordination of a Bishop, of Priests, and of Deacons*, 115. The mention of the Seven serving at table provides a parallel to the Levites' ministry at the "former tabernacle."

21. Susan K. Wood, *Sacramental Orders*, Lex Orandi (Collegeville, MN: The Liturgical Press, 2000), 157–58. The tasks of word, liturgy and charity, which the deacon performs "showing himself servant of all," are to be covered in the homily, *Rites of Ordination of a Bishop, of Priests, and of Deacons*, 106–7.

22. Wood, *Sacramental Orders*, 157–58.

23. Margaret Morche, *Zur Erneuerung des Ständigen Diakonats* (Freiburg: Lambertus, 1996), esp. 15–21, 36–62.

24. Paul Winninger, immediately after the council, writes of Christ the servant as the key to the deacon's "spirituality," in *Les diacres. Histoire et avenir du diaconat* (Paris: Centurion, 1967), 131–37. Patrick McCaslin and Michael G. Lawler, in *Sacrament of Service: A Vision of the Permanent Diaconate Today* (New York: Paulist Press, 1986), develop a broad and variegated view of service based on early empirical studies of the diaconal ministry in the United States.

170

25. Vorgrimler, "Liturgie, Diakonie, und Diakone."

26. Reiner Kaczynski, "'...non ad sacerdotium, sed ad ministerium.' Überlegungen zum Diakonat," in Kraneman, Sternberg, and Zahner, *Die Diakonale Dimension der Liturgie*, 220–35. Christian Delarbre, "Diaconat et épiscopat," insists on rooting the deacon's ministry in that of the bishop and expresses reservations about the model of Christ the servant (see chapter 8 below), but sees charitable service as the defining mark of the diaconal ministry.

27. Two writers who do pick up this theme: William T. Ditewig, *The Emerging Diaconate: Servant Leaders in a Servant Church* (New York: Paulist Press, 2007), 126–28, 136–38, insists that deacons must be agents of ongoing renewal in the Church; and see Robert Zollitch, "Der Diakonat - ein modernes Amt," in *Bereit wozu? Geweiht für was? Zur Diskussion um den Ständigen Diakonat*, ed. Klemens Armbruster and Matthias Mühl, Quaestiones Disputatae 232 (Freiburg: Herder, 2009), 374.

28. See, e.g., the strong "servant" focus in Pope Francis's homily at the diaconate jubilee, May 29, 2016: https://w2.vatican.va/content/francesco/it/homilies/2016/documents/papa-francesco_20160529_omelia-giubileo-diaconi.html. Particularly after the ITC raised its questions about Christ the servant in 2003, however, Church documents have been more cautious in appealing specifically to "Christ the servant," a development noted by Christian Delarbre, "Diaconat et épiscopat. Pour éviter une approche sacerdotale du diaconat," *Nouvelle revue théologique* 133 (2011/12): 238–40.

29. John N. Collins, *Diakonia: Re-interpreting the Ancient Sources* (New York: Oxford, 1990); more recently, "The Problem with Values Carried by Diakonia/Diakonie in Recent Church Documents," in *Diakonia Studies* (New York: Oxford, 2014), 37–56.

30. ITC, *Le diaconat*, 7(b) (E.T., 95–96). Despite these cautions, the ITC states in its conclusion (after 7[d]), together with other rather tentative considerations, that the deacon is a "living icon of Christ the servant," quoting the *Basic Norms for the Formation of Permanent Deacons* discussed above.

31. Noted by Christian Delarbre, "Diaconat et épiscopat," 238.

32. A web search of diaconate vocation offices, formation programs, and associations around the world reveals (in URLs far too numerous to cite here) that when ministerial identity is directly addressed, apart from canonical, logistical, and functional questions, the servant framework, and often the image of Christ the servant, make up by far the most common theme. In the United States, the National Association of Diaconate Directors' three-day conference in July, 2018, celebrating the fiftieth

anniversary of the diaconate in America, was titled "Christ the Servant: Yesterday, Today, Forever." A recent treatment of diaconal vocation, formation, and ministry by one of the most widely read writers on the diaconate in English uses Christ the servant as its unquestioned framework: see James Keating, *The Heart of the Diaconate: Communion with the Servant Mysteries of Christ* (New York: Paulist Press, 2015). Examples could be multiplied greatly.

33. Examples: Walter Kasper, *Leadership in the Church*, trans. Brian McNeil (New York: Crossroad, 2003), 13–44; Michael Evans, "The Deacon: Icon of Christ the Servant," *Pastoral Review* (July–August 2006): 28–32; Zollitch, "Der Diakonat – ein modernes Amt," in *Bereit wozu? Geweiht für was?*, 372–80; Johannes Kreidler, "Systematisch-theologische Grundfragen im Zusammenhang mit der kirchenamt-lichen Lehre," in *Ortsbestimmungen: Der Diakonat als kirchlicher Dienst*, ed. Richard Hartmann, Franz Reger, and Stefan Sander (Frankfurt am Main: Josef Knecht, 2009), 59–69.

CHAPTER SEVEN

1. For example, R. Pagé, *Diaconat permanent et diversité des ministères*, Perspectives du Droit Canonique (Montreal, 1988), 61. Quoted and cited in ITC, *Le diaconat*, 6(c) (E.T., 88).

2. This way of defining the theology of ministry as applied to deacons combines Richard Gaillardetz's view of ministry as "ecclesial re-positioning" (see below in this chapter), focusing on a minister's pattern of relationships in the Church, with an appreciation of the way in which actual ministerial tasks or services come to define who the minister is. See Richard Gaillardetz, "The Ecclesiological Foundations of Ministry within an Ordered Communion," in *Ordering the Baptismal Priesthood: Theologies of Lay and Ordained Ministry*, ed. Susan Wood (Collegeville, MN: The Liturgical Press, 2003), 26–51, esp. 36–41; and Kathleen Cahalan, *Introducing the Practice of Ministry* (Collegeville, MN: The Liturgical Press, 2010), 48–67.

3. As discussed in chapter 4, the leadership role is somewhat expanded in *AG* 16 (deacons are *moderantes*), but it is still exercised under supervision.

4. United States Conference of Catholic Bishops, *National Directory for the Formation, Ministry, and Life of Permanent Deacons* (Washington, DC: USCCB, 2005), 20–21.

5. Benedict XVI, *Omnium in Mentem* (October 26, 2009), http://

w2.vatican.va/content/benedict-xvi/en/apost_letters/documents/
hf_ben-xvi_apl_20091026_codex-iuris-canonici.html.

6. The framework of *LG* 29 is developed in Congregation for Catholic Education, *Ratio Fundamentalis Institutionum Diaconorum Permanentium* (1998), no. 9, http://www.vatican.va/roman _curia/congregations/ccatheduc/documents/rc_con_ccatheduc _doc_31031998_directorium-diaconi_lt.html, which defines the third task as follows: "Finally, the task of governing is performed through a commitment to the works of charity and assistance and for the benefit of communities or areas of ecclesial life, especially as regards charitable activities. This is the ministry most characteristic of the deacon."

7. William Ditewig, "The Kenotic Leadership of Deacons," in *The Deacon Reader*, ed. James Keating (New York: Paulist Press, 2006), 248-77.

8. For an empirical study of diaconal functions in the United States, see Center for Applied Research in the Apostolate [CARA], *Word, Liturgy, Charity: The Diaconate in the U.S. Catholic Church, 1968-2018* (Lanham, MD: Lexington Books, 2018), 81-100. A recent series from Liturgical Press provides a combination of theological and practical treatments: Jay Cormier, *The Deacon's Ministry of the Word* (2016); Frederick C. Bauerschmidt, *The Deacon's Ministry of the Liturgy* (2016); and William T. Ditewig, *The Deacon's Ministry of Charity and Justice* (Collegeville, MN: The Liturgical Press, 2015).

9. The shifting emphases over time between liturgical, charitable, and catechetical roles for deacons in Germany is well summarized by Stefan Sander, "Anlass and Zielsetzung des Symposions," in *Ortsbestimmungen: Der Diakonat als kirchlicher Dienst*, ed. Richard Hartmann, Franz Reger, and Stephan Sander (Frankfurt am Main: Josef Knecht, 2009), 6. For the United States, see the CARA study cited above (n. 8), 81-99.

10. Thus, Richard Gaillardetz defines diaconal ministry as "service to the ministry of *episkopē*," in "On the Theological Integrity of the Diaconate," in *Theology of the Diaconate: The State of the Question*, ed. Owen F. Cummings, William T. Ditewig, and Richard R. Gaillardetz (New York: Paulist Press, 2005), 67-97.

11. Rupert M. Scheule argues that since all of the functions of deacons could in principle be performed by a nonordained person (actually, this is not true of certain liturgical roles), the key to diaconal identity must be sought elsewhere than in functions, specifically in the deacon's character as an ordained minister living mainly in a non-Church setting: "Ja zum vagen Amt. Apologie eines offenen theologischen Selbsverständnisses Ständiger Diakone," in Hartmann, Reger,

and Sander, *Ortsbestimmungen*, 70-77. The deacon's typical social location is an enabling factor in his identity as minister of the threshold (see chapter 9 below), but the office itself has defined functions that give that ministry its contours in those settings.

12. *LG* 21, Tanner, 2:865, lines 15-21.

13. Didier Gonneaud argues correctly that defining diaconal ministry as participation in the bishop's office undermines the diaconate's sacramentality as well as its distinctiveness: "La sacramentalité du ministère diaconale," *Revue théologique de Louvain* 36 (2005): 3-20 at 5-7.

14. Gaillardetz, "The Ecclesiological Foundations of Ministry," 36-38.

15. This statement is true of vowed religious who are not ordained, not with respect to their vows (if permanent and public), but with respect to any offices they may hold within or outside their religious community, since the offices are not permanent and sacramental as ordained ministry is.

16. Or different from bishops and priests for that matter, unless it could be shown that one sacramental character was referred on all those who receive holy orders. See the next section of this chapter. On a relational ontology see Gaillardetz, "The Ecclesiological Foundations of Ministry," 38-41.

17. See *Rites of Ordination of a Bishop, of Priests, and of Deacons*: three tasks in the homily, 106-7, and also in the Prayer of Ordination, 116; obedience and service, 109-11.

18. *Rites of Ordination of a Bishop, of Priests, and of Deacons*, 116.

19. One could also say, with Didier Gonneaud, that there is only one configuration to Christ, in baptism; through confirmation and each of the three grades of order, this configuration would be given a new and specific direction. See "La sacramentalité du ministère diaconal," 10-11. This book's account of diaconal identity and of its sacramentality is consistent with Gonneaud's formulation.

20. Alphonse Borras, *Le diaconat au risque de sa nouveauté* (Brussels: Lessius, 2007), 111-49, criticizes a diaconal configuration to Christ generally, and a christological understanding of sacramental character specifically, on several grounds. However, the idea of configuration can withstand these criticisms if properly qualified as it is here.

21. For a summary of patristic understandings of sacramental representation and later developments, with references, see *Oxford Dictionary of the Christian Church*, ed. F. L. Cross and E. A. Livingstone, 3rd ed. (New York: Oxford University Press, 2005), s.v. "Sacrament."

22. *To the Trallians* 3.1.

23. Service to the *ekklēsia*, *To the Trallians* 2.3. Service to the bishop is repeatedly stressed for everyone but especially for deacons, e.g. *To the Magnesians* 2.1.

24. The *Catechism* at 1570 identifies Christ the servant as the character imprinted on deacons at ordination, but the *Directorium* of 1998 makes no reference to this (see nos. 44, 47) and the ITC in 2003 notes the *Catechism* passage without any explicit endorsement (*Le diaconat*, 7[b], E.T., 93). Even if we accept the *Catechism*'s definition of sacramental character for deacons as stated, we are still able to define a fuller ministerial identity for deacons (including, as in this book, servant and threshold dimensions) and show that identity to have a broadly sacramental aspect. See chapters 8 and 9.

25. Summary by Dorothea Sattler, "Charakter, Sakramentaler," in *Lexikon für Theologie und Kirche*. 11 vols. (Freiburg: Herder, 1994), 2:1009–13, with references; Barrett, "Ordination," 66–67, 73–76, and 78–79, on the evolving definition of character in holy orders.

26. Herbert Vorgrimler, *Sacramental Theology*, trans. Linda Moloney (Collegeville, MN: Liturgical Press, 1992), 263–65, 274–76.

27. This list is not exhaustive but covers the major terms used. All have been employed in works quoted or cited in this book.

28. *Ratio Fundamentalis*, 5 and 11.

29. For issues regarding the deacon "acting in the person of Christ [the servant]," see, for background, Anthony Barrett, "What Is Ordination? A Roman Catholic Perspective," *Ecclesiology* 3, no. 1(2006): 57–79; medieval origins at 67–68, issues regarding priesthood at 75. Specifically on the diaconate, see Alphonse Borras, *Le diaconat au risque*, 131–49, and Christian Delarbre, "Diaconat et épiscopat," 236–41.

CHAPTER EIGHT

1. "Christ the servant" is a metaphor and can also be called an image, in that it combines attributes of a person/situation so that a mental picture may be formed. The metaphor or image is termed a model or an example when its content is being applied to another person or situation (here, Christ the servant is applied particularly to diaconal identity).

2. John Byron, "Servant," in *The New Interpreter's Dictionary of the Bible*, 5 vols. (Nashville: Abingdon Press, 2009), 5:192, with references.

3. Byron, "Servant," 192, and the article following by Raymond F. Collins, "Servant of the Lord," 192–95.

4. The first three aspects of the image of Christ the servant below use Dulles's specific questions about the servant Church in *Models of the Church*, expanded ed. (New York: Doubleday, 2002), 91–92.

5. Phil 2:5–8; Matt 12:18–21 (=Isa 42:1–4) and Isa 52:13—53:13 as a frame for the Synoptic passion narratives. Stanley Porter, *Sacred Tradition in the New Testament* (Grand Rapid: Baker Academic, 2016), 79–104.

6. Matt 4:23; 12:28; Luke 9:1–2; 10:8–9. The healings in John's Gospel are signs that point to God's full self-revelation (e.g. 4:54; 6:2; 12:18). In a further development, the healings and distributions of goods performed by the apostles after Pentecost are signs of the spread of the gospel through the power of the Holy Spirit. See the discussion of Acts 6:1–6 in chapter 2 and appendix 1.

7. See Holly Beers, *The Followers of Jesus as the 'Servant': Luke's Model from Isaiah for the Disciples in Luke–Acts*, Library of New Testament Studies 535 (London: Bloomsbury T&T Clark, 2015).

8. *LG* 18, Tanner 2:862, lines 36–38.

9. The deacon's roles in administering baptism, blessing marriages, and leading groups in prayer, including at funerals or benediction, are not inherently presiding roles, as they do not gather the community in the way that the Eucharist does. These roles are also delegated or overseen by pastors. This distinction undermines the critique of Sherri L. Vallee, "The Restoration of the Permanent Diaconate: A Blending of Roles," *Worship* 77, no. 6 (2003): 530–32.

10. A deacon administering a parish under canon 517.2 is not performing an inherently diaconal function, but exercising an office that can also be performed by a layperson. The same can be said of parish or diocesan staff roles that may happen to be exercised by deacons.

11. For example, ITC, *Le diaconat*, 7(b) (E.T., 95–96); "On the Theological Integrity of the Diaconate," in *Theology of the Diaconate: The State of the Question*, ed. Owen F. Cummings, William T. Ditewig, and Richard R. Gaillardetz (New York: Paulist Press, 2005), 73.

12. For example, Gaillardetz, "Theological Integrity," 72–73.

13. For example, Stefan Sander, *Das Amt des Diakons*, 2nd ed. (Freiburg im Breisgau: Herder, 2008), 137–38.

14. Gerhard Kittel, ed., *Theological Dictionary of the New Testament*, trans. Geoffrey W. Bromiley, 10 vols. (Grand Rapids: Wm. B. Eerdmans, 1964); Beyer entries are at 2:81–93. Discussion by John N.

Collins, *Deacons and the Church: Making Connections between Old and New* (Harrisburg, PA: Morehouse, 2002), 1-14.

15. John N. Collins, *Diakonia: Re-interpreting the Ancient Sources* (New York: Oxford, 1990), 254. Collins's conclusions were incorporated into revised entries in Frederick W. Danker, ed., *A Greek-English Lexicon of the New Testament and Other Early Christian Literature*, 3rd ed. (Chicago: University of Chicago Press, 2000), s.v. *diakonos* 2, where Collins's study is quoted. This lexicon is cited hereafter as BDAG 3rd. ed.

16. For example, Collins, *Deacons and the Church*, and *Diakonia Studies: Critical Issues in Ministry* (New York: Oxford University Press, 2014), 165-264, incorporating writings from the previous decade. Robert Zollitch, "Der Diakonat - ein modernes Amt," in *Bereit wozu? Geweiht für was? Zur Diskussion um den Ständigen Diakonat*, ed. Klemens Armbruster and Matthias Mühl, Quaestiones Disputatae 232 (Freiburg: Herder, 2009) accepts Collins's argument that the *diakon*-words define a deacon as one who is sent or commissioned, and then moves effortlessly to say that deacons are sent out to be a sign of Christ the servant and of the servant Church.

17. It may be enough to say, with Stefan Sander, that the Church has broad freedom to change the content of ministerial offices, but "reviving" the diaconate within the framework of "Christ the servant" actually followed a New Testament model of development—see below. Stefan Sander, "Anlass and Zielsetzung des Symposions," in *Ortsbestimmungen: Der Diakonat als kirchlicher Dienst*, ed. Richard Hartmann, Franz Reger, and Stephan Sander (Frankfurt am Main: Josef Knecht, 2009), 6.

18. Alistair Stewart has argued (*The Original Bishops* [Grand Rapids: Baker Academic, 2014], 100-19) that food distribution in connection with community meals was a function of *diakonoi* in the earliest churches, an adaptation of the role of *diakonoi* within fraternal associations. Thus the original understanding of *diakonos* as an office may have had more of an inherent charitable dimension than Collins suggests.

19. Collins, *Deacons and the Church*, 119-20.

20. Collins, *Deacons and the Church*, 134.

21. Collins, *Deacons and the Church*, 131. Collins's use of the term *commemorative meal* rather than *Eucharist* is consistent with the ecumenical framework of his argument.

CHAPTER NINE

1. Christian Wesseley, *Gekommen, um zu dienen. Der Diakonat aus fundamentaltheologisch-ekklesiologischer Sicht* (Regensburg: Friedrich Pustet, 2004), esp. 223–25; Hans-Joachim Sander, "Diakonat: die heterotope Dimension des kirklichen Amtes," in *Ortsbestimmungen: Der Diakonat als kirchlicher Dienst*, ed. Richard Hartmann, Franz Reger, and Stephan Sander (Frankfurt am Main: Josef Knecht, 2009); Stefan Sander, *Gott begegnet im Anderen. Der Diakon und die Einheit des sakramentalen Amtes* (Freiburg: Herder, 2006), 261–304.

2. The in-between aspect of the threshold itself has been developed metaphorically, particularly by anthropologists, using the Latin *limen* for threshold, in the idea of liminality, characterizing a threshold place or experience that is on the edge of what is known and defined, and therefore has a certain ambiguity and openness to encounter. W. Shawn McKnight, *Understanding the Diaconate: Historical, Theological, and Sociological Foundations* (Washington, DC: The Catholic University of America Press, 2018), 175–202, applies the idea of liminality specifically to the deacon's role at Mass. This approach, along with McKnight's broader argument about the deacon as a mediating figure, primarily within the Church community, overlap with some aspects the threshold model developed here.

3. These two poles are present in all four Gospels; the movement from margin to center is a structuring principle in Luke's narrative.

4. After the second use of this expression, Jesus actually moves outside Israel to heal the daughter of the Syrophoenician woman.

5. Implicit throughout the Gospel and frequently explicit as well, e.g. John 1:14; 13:3; 16:28.

6. For a classic account of "inaugurated eschatology," see Dale C. Allison Jr., *The End of the Ages Has Come* (Philadelphia: Fortress Press, 1985). For the integration of this perspective into the Fourth Gospel, see Tim O'Donnell, "Complementary Eschatologies in John 5:19–30," *Catholic Biblical Quarterly* 70, no. 4 (2008): 736–51.

7. Francois Lepargneur, "Ein Diakonat für Lateinamerika," in *Diaconia in Christo*, 476.

8. Henri Denis, "Le diaconat dans la hiérarchie," in *Diacre*, 148.

CHAPTER TEN

1. *LG* 18, Tanner, 2:862, lines 35–39.

2. This is not to suggest that the priest or pastor should be strongly identified with the community's "in-crowd," or indeed has any less of a mission to its margins. However, the pastor/presider also strongly represents the gathered community in a way that deacons do not; moreover, deacons in their social location live at the threshold of Church and world. Thus, deacons represent a ministry of the threshold much more intensely than priests and pastors (including bishops).

CHAPTER ELEVEN

1. 45,600 as of December 31, 2016. 73.3 percent of the world's diocesan deacons are from Europe and North America. The percentage was even higher in 1973: 83.8 percent. *Statistical Yearbook of the Church* 2016, 92–100; 1987, 86–93. The rising percentage of deacons outside the Western context points to the possibility of other typical contexts. However, these would need have a unifying set of characteristics, developed somehow from the wide variety of conditions in Latin America, Asia, Africa, and Oceania, in order to become a typical ministerial context like the Western one defined here. It is not enough to propose a typical case simply as one covering all of the regions where the diaconate is lightly planted, as the ITC does in *Le diaconat*, 6(a) (E.T., 80–82).

2. The parallel diaconates are longstanding among the Orthodox and are currently the norm in the Anglican communion as well.

3. *Ministeria quaedam*, August 15, 1972, *AAS* (1972): 529–34. For discussion of the issue for the diaconate, see Susan K. Wood, *Sacramental Orders*, Lex Orandi (Collegeville, MN: The Liturgical Press, 2000), 166–71.

4. The minority of deacons who work professionally in parish or diocesan positions are not strictly exercising their diaconal ministry in those positions, which could be filled by someone who is not a deacon, while the deacon is typically exercising diaconal ministry outside the Church employment as well.

5. *AG* 16, Tanner, 2:1026, lines 7–8.

6. CARA, *Word, Liturgy, Charity*, 39–40, reports that in 2017 146 U.S. parishes were administered by deacons under Canon 517.2, providing a decidedly atypical (0.8 percent) ministry role among approximately 18,000 U.S. deacons. The number of deacons administering parishes has remained basically unchanged since 2004, even as the number of deacons has increased dramatically.

7. The literature on both sides of this issue is extensive, and the brief summary of arguments cannot do full justice to them. But the point here is to show that the debate neither affects nor is affected by the ministerial identity defined in this book. For the arguments from authority and the unity of Orders, see, e.g., Gerhard Müller, *Priesthood and Diaconate: The Recipient of the Sacrament of Holy Orders from the Perspective of Creation Theology and Eschatology*, trans. Michael J. Miller (San Francisco, CA: Ignatius Press, 2002), 35–62, 183–226. For the iconic argument, see Sara Butler, "Women Deacons and Sacramental Symbolism," *New Diaconal Review* 6 (2011): 38–49.

8. See, e.g., Gary Macy, William T. Ditewig, and Phyllis Zagano, *Women Deacons: Past, Present, Future* (New York: Paulist Press, 2011). The ITC does not take a definitive position on the question: *Le diaconat*, conclusion (E.T. 109–10).

9. Worldwide, there were 703 permanent deacons in religious orders in 2016, only 1.5 percent of the world's deacons. The number of religious order deacons is increasing, but the percentage relative to the whole diaconate is declining. *Statistical Manual of the Church*: 1987, 86–93; 2016, 92–100.

10. CARA, *Word, Liturgy, Charity*, 84–86, reports that in 2017 26 percent of active deacons in the United States worked in full- or part-time compensated ministry positions, 11 percent in full-time positions. The total percentage of U.S. deacons in compensated ministry is unchanged since 2001.

APPENDIX ONE

1. A recent exhaustive commentary in which the traditional identification of the Seven as deacons is never mentioned: Craig S. Keener, *Acts: An Exegetical Commentary*, 2 vols. (Grand Rapids: Baker, 2013), 2: 1247–93. Likewise, Luke T. Johnson, *The Acts of the Apostles*, Sacra Pagina 5 (Collegeville, MN: The Liturgical Press, 1992), 104–6.

2. For example, Joseph Fitzmyer (*The Acts of the Apostles*, Anchor Bible 31 [New York: Doubleday, 1992], 345) says that the office of deacon "developed from" the Seven, but notes problems with tracing that development and refers to other scholarly treatments that argue against his own assertion.

3. For example, William S. Kurz, *Acts of the Apostles*, Catholic Commentary on Sacred Scripture (Grand Rapids: Baker Academic, 2013), 109–13.

4. See BDAG 3rd ed., s.v. *diakoneō* 5; Collins, *Diakonia*, 230-31.

5. John N. Collins, *Deacons and the Church: Making Connections between Old and New* (Harrisburg, PA: Morehouse, 2002), 47-58 argues that *diakonia* is Luke's "code word" for preaching and evangelizing. He comes to the interesting conclusion that the *diakonia* for which the Seven are commissioned here is not the care of any physical needs, but rather preaching in Greek to the widows at home ("at tables"), since they are unable to come into the temple precinct, and if there would not understand the Aramaic preaching of the Twelve. Given the importance of meals (Acts 2:42) and of the common fund (Acts 2:44-46; 4:32-37) in the apostolic *diakonia* described in Acts 2—5, however, the "at tables," here a dative of respect, seems more likely to be referring specifically to tables where food or money is distributed, rather than by implication to the homes of the widows.

6. Irenaeus, *Epideixis Adversus Haereses*, 1.26.3, 3.12.10, 4.15.1., ed. Norbert Brox, Fontes Christiani 8, 5 vols. (Freiburg: Herder, 1993), 1:316, 3:346, 4:112.

7. See, e.g., Alistair Stewart, *The Original Bishops* (Grand Rapids: Baker Academic, 2014), 100-19, with references.

8. John Chrysostom, *In Acta Apostolorum* 14, in J. P. Migne, *Patrologiae cursus completus...Series graeca* (Paris, 1857-66), 60:116.

9. See also Acts 1:17, 25; 21:19 for *diakonia* meaning the apostolic ministry as a whole.

APPENDIX TWO

1. See 1 Cor 12:4-31; Rom 12:6-7; Eph 4:11, and chapter 2 above.

2. See Abraham J. Malherbe, *Moral Exhortation: A Greco-Roman Sourcebook*, Library of Early Christianity (Philadelphia: Westminster, 1986), 138-41; also Martin Dibelius and Hans Conzelmann, *The Pastoral Epistles: A Commentary on Pastoral Epistles*, trans. Philip Buttolph and Adela Yarbro, Hermeneia (Philadelphia: Fortress Press, 1972), 158-60 for the text of Onosander on the qualities of a good general.

3. The meaning of the phrase "husband of one wife" has been debated widely. It may denote simply marital fidelity, or describe a man who does not remarry after being widowed or divorced, or refer to a man in a faithful monogamous relationship as opposed to being unmarried. Since this passage aims to exhort rather than regulate, the basic point (whatever the details) is that the man's marriage should be blameless.

4. The interpretation of this line has been debated extensively. The main questions are (1) whether the women are deacons themselves or wives of deacons and (2) if they are deacons, whether they hold the same office or have the same functions as the men. Besides the commentaries, see Judith Stiefel, "Women Deacons in 1 Timothy: A Linguistic and Literary Look at 'Women Likewise...' (1 Tim 3:11)" *New Testament Studies* 41 (1995): 442-51.

5. The main doctrinal issues are speculations about law (1:3-11) and an ascetic teaching that forbids marriage and certain foods (4:1-5).

6. For a close study of the verbal parallels and other literary techniques, see Ray Van Neste, *Cohesion and Structure in the Pastoral Epistles,* Journal for the Study of the New Testament Supplement 280 (London: T&T Clark, 2004), 86-87.

APPENDIX THREE

1. John N. Collins, *Diakonia: Re-interpreting the Ancient Sources* (New York: Oxford, 1990).

2. BDAG 3rd ed, s.v. *diakonos* 2, where Collins's study is quoted.

3. John Byron, "Servant," in *The New Interpreter's Dictionary of the Bible,* 5 vols. (Nashville: Abington, 2009), 5:192. BDAG 3rd ed., s.vv. *diakoneo/ diakonia/ diakonos; douleia/ douleuō/ doulē/ doulos; pais* 3.

4. Christ as *doulos:* Phil 2:7. Ministers of the gospel as *douloi:* Rom 1:1; 2 Cor 4:5; Gal 1:10; Titus 1:1; Jas 1:1; 2 Pet 1:1. This list is illustrative, but far from exhaustive. The word *pais* in various Scripture passages contributes to the metaphor of Christ the servant, but does not add another dimension to the servant metaphor for our purposes here.

INDEX

Index

camp, 30; deacons as ordained members of, 26, 38, 81, 85, 110; deacons' role within, 59–61, 63, 71, 93–94, 99, 107–8; diaconate as "bridge" role between laity and, 3, 34, 37–38, 53, 65–67, 99, 112; Eucharist role of, 63, 67, 69; *Lumen Gentium* and, 50–53; marriage and, 34–35, 45, 63; missionary churches and, 47; revival of diaconate and, 30; in Roman Catholic Church, 55–58; as servants, 57–58, 91; service of, 35–37, 44, 56–57, 65, 72, 74; tasks of, 59, 75, 78, 93; Vatican II's views of, 34–35, 46. *See also specific name*

Clericalism, 55
Code of Canon Law (1917), 51, 75
Collegiality, 43–44, 48–49
Collins, John N., 71–72, 94–98, 150–52
Colson, Jean, 12
Conference on the Apostolate of the Laity, 32
Confirmation, 69, 79, 128
Congar, Yves, 66–67
Congregation for Catholic Education, 69
Council of Trent, 26
Croce, Walter, 12
Culture and diaconate, 9, 119, 123

Dachau concentration camp, 30
"Deacon words," 97, 150–52
Decree on Missionary Activity. See *Ad Gentes*
Denis, Henri, 67
de Smedt, Bishop Emiel-Jozef, 55
Diaconal ministry. *See* Diaconate

Diaconate: anomalies in status quo of (mid-twentieth century), 26–29; "bridge" role between Eucharist and ordinary life and, 131; "bridge" role between higher clergy and laity, 3, 34, 37–38, 53, 65–67, 99, 112; challenge to, contemporary, 134–36; collaboration with priests and, 121–22; culture and, 9, 119, 123; Denis and, 67; early Church and, 10–11; everyday reality of, 111–12; fragmentation surrounding, 5–6; geographical context of, 1, 8–9; growth in, 1; institutional context of, 7–9, 118–19; invisibility of, 2; laity and, 122–23; leadership of, 24, 57, 59–60, 75–76, 93, 95, 98, 122, 126, 131; marriage and, 8, 10, 29, 34–35, 45, 49, 119; as minipriests, 64–65, 137; missionary churches and, 47; New Testament and, 14; obedience promise of, 80–81, 85, 88, 116, 122; *parrhesia* and, 149; Paul VI's sanction of, 1; as reformist movement, 35–36; Roman Catholic permanent, 98; secular jobs and, 8; as servants, 54–58; service and, 2–3; service of, 2–3, 37, 40, 44, 54, 71, 81–82, 85, 95–98, 110, 112, 121–22, 131–32, 135; shortage of priests and, 8, 30–31, 65, 118, 136–37; social profile of priests and, 137–38; tasks of, 3, 17, 19, 24, 70, 75–76, 81, 85, 95, 108–9, 113, 119–20,

185

Index

Praise for *The Deacon*

Deacon Tim O'Donnell's book provides an accessible overview of the theological foundations of the diaconate and the distinctive quality of the deacons' ministry. One of the great achievements of the Second Vatican Council was to lift up for us the Order of Deacons and the treasures that this vocation can bring to our Church. I highly recommend Deacon O'Donnell's book, which provides Catholics and all those seeking to learn more about the work of the Church with a thoughtful and enlightening understanding of diaconal ministry.

—*Cardinal Seán O'Malley, OFMCap., Archbishop of Boston*

Superb. Deacon Tim O'Donnell gives us a clear and comprehensive vision of the diaconate that helps us all see our ministry with new eyes. Drawing on history, theology, scholarship, and practical experience, he offers an important work that should be a part of every deacon's—and, for that matter, every priest's—library.

—*Deacon Greg Kandra, journalist and blogger,*
"The Deacon's Bench"

Tim O'Donnell's accessible yet meticulously researched book makes a much needed contribution to contemporary ecclesiology and the ministerial life of the Church today. The permanent diaconate represents one of the most important developments to emerge out of the Second Vatican Council. And yet, with over 46,000 permanent deacons worldwide, almost half of whom minister in North America, it has remained, in many ways, a ministry in search of a theology. O'Donnell offers a coherent and compelling theological account of the distinctive contribution that permanent deacons offer the Church. This book will be of immense value to theologians interested in a theology of ministry, those involved in diaconal formation and, most of all, those engaged in diaconal ministry in service of the Church today.

—*Richard R. Gaillardetz, Joseph Professor of Catholic Systematic Theology, Boston College*

By calling upon his decades of research on the permanent diaconate and on his own experience as a deacon, Tim O'Donnell clarifies what the permanent diaconate is, what its ideals are, and how it functions in today's Church. The book fills an embarrassing gap in our understanding of ministry today. It will be indispensable reading for bishops, priests, and deacons, and enlightening reading for all of us.

—*John W. O'Malley. SJ, University Professor, Georgetown University*

Who are these deacons? As one involved in diaconate formation for over a decade, I greatly appreciate Tim O'Donnell's crafting of a book integrating historical and theological perspectives with current ministerial experience. A thorough and quality melding of scholarship and formative reflection on the reemergence of those called to service and bridge-building!

—*Monica Verploegen, PhD, Co-Founder / Retreat Director, Tatenda International*

This is the book we have been waiting for. Deacon Tim O'Donnell writes elegantly and comprehensively. He fully justifies his claim to work out a theologically coherent and pastorally applicable understanding of the distinctive identity of the order of deacons—who they are, what they do, and what is distinctive about them. His investigation of sources is remarkably wide-ranging: ordination rites; the New Testament; patristic, medieval, and Tridentine sources; papal and other teaching documents; the Second Vatican Council; and the contributions of theologians before, during, and since the Council. Particularly valuable is his ability to draw the major French, German, and Italian writers on the diaconate into conversation with American and other English-language theologians. This promises to be the definitive book on the subject for at least a generation. It will be indispensable for those involved in the formation of deacons and for scholars of sacramental theology and ecclesiology, while being completely accessible to deacons and diaconate candidates as well.

—*Deacon Tony Schmitz, Director of Studies, Bishops Conference of Scotland Diaconate Commission*

Decades after the restoration of the permanent diaconate, Deacon O'Donnell provides a much needed theological clarification of its specific nature and purpose: as the model of a distinctive Christian ministry of service to others, and of creative presence and outreach to all who are on the peripheries of society and the Church.

—*Msgr. Charles Murphy, STD, Founding Director of the Permanent Diaconate, Diocese of Portland, Maine*